Christopher Middleton was ~~born~~ in Cornwall in 1926. He studied at Merton College, Oxford ... ~~litera~~ture at King's College, London, and since ... He has received many awa... ...an and his original work.

C000180781

By the same author

111 Poems
Serpentine
Two Horse Wagon Going By
The Pursuit of the Kingfisher: essays

Selected translations

Friedrich Nietzsche, *Selected Letters*
Robert Walser, *Jakob von Gunten, Selected Stories*
Elias Canetti, *Kafka's Other Trial*
Goethe, *Selected Poems*
Gert Hofmann, *The Spectacle at the Tower,*
   Our Conquest, The Parable of the Blind,
   Balzac's Horse and Other Stories

CHRISTOPHER MIDDLETON

Selected Writings

PALADIN
GRAFTON BOOKS
A Division of the Collins Publishing Group

LONDON GLASGOW
TORONTO SYDNEY AUCKLAND

Paladin
Grafton Books
A Division of the Collins Publishing Group
8 Grafton Street, London W1X 3LA

Published in Paladin Books 1990

First published in Great Britain by
Carcanet Press Ltd 1989

Copyright © Christopher Middleton 1962, 1965, 1969,
1975, 1977, 1980, 1983, 1985, 1986, 1989

ISBN 0-586-08751-6

Printed and bound in Great Britain by
Collins, Glasgow

Set in Times

All rights reserved. No part of this publication
may be reproduced, stored in a retrieval system,
or transmitted, in any form, or by any means,
electronic, mechanical, photocopying, recording or
otherwise, without the prior permission of
the publishers.

This book is sold subject to the condition that
it shall not, by way of trade or otherwise, be
lent, re-sold, hired out or otherwise circulated
without the publisher's prior consent in any
form of binding or cover other than that
in which it is published and without a similar
condition including this condition being
imposed on the subsequent purchaser.

Acknowledgements
Grateful acknowledgement is made to Oasis Books,
London, for permission to reprint eight sections from
Serpentine, and to the editors of the following journals:
Antaeus (New York) for 'Cybele'; *Numbers* (Cambridge,
England) for 'Another Almost' and 'From Earth
Myriad Robed'; *PN Review* for 'Michèle's Rooms',
'Cybele', 'The China Virgins', 'The First Move', and
'A Farewell in Old Mexico'.

Contents

3

Poems from *The Lonely Suppers of W.V. Balloon* (1975) and
Carminalenia (1980)

6
Poems and Prose 1986-7

7
From *The Pursuit of the Kingfisher* (1983)

1

Poems from *Torse 3* (1962), *Nonsequences* (1965)
and *Our Flowers & Nice Bones* (1969)

At Porthcothan

A speck of dark at low tide on the tideline,
It could not be identified as any known thing,
Until, as one approached, a neck was clear
(It is agreed that logs, or cans, are neckless),
And then a body, over which the neck stood
Curved like a questionmark, emerged
As oval, and the whole shape was crouching
Helpless in a small pool the sea had left.

The oval body, with green sheen as of pollen
Shading off into the black plumage, and the neck
Surmounted by the tiny wide-eyed head,
Were not without beauty. The head was moving,
So like a cobra it seemed rash to offer
An introductory finger to the long hooked bill
Stabbing the air. Danger had so
Sharpened what intelligence the bird possessed,
It seemed to pierce the mind of the observer.
In fact we were afraid, yes afraid of each other.

Finally though I picked it up and took it
To a quiet side-bay where dogs were rarer.
Here the shag sat, happy in the sun,
Perched on a slab of rock where a pool was,
In which I caught five fish for it
With a pocketknife, a handkerchief
And a plunging forefinger. But at six o'clock
It left the rock and waddled off seaward.

Though breakers came in high and curling
It straddled them, bouncing, buoyant,
Borne alone the sealine sideways, with head up,
Slithering across the bay's whole width, and then
Drifted ashore again, to scuttle flapping
With webbed feet flat like a Saturday banker's
To shelter on a level rock. Here it studied,
With the air of one of whom something is expected,
The turbulent Atlantic slowly rising.
What could I do but leave it meditating?

Early next morning, on the bay's north side,
I found it cuddled under the cliff. The tide
Was low again. What hungry darkness
Had driven so the dark young shag to shelter?
It did not resist when I picked it up.
Something had squeezed the cobra out of it.

I took it to a cave where the sun shone in,
Then caught two fish. It opened one green eye,
And then another. But though I cut
The fish into portions, presenting these
To the bill's hooked tip, it only shook its head.
Noon came. The shag slept in the cave. At two
I hurried back. The shag was stone dead,
With its fine glossy head laid back a little
Over the left shoulder, and a few flies
Were pestering its throat and the fish scraps
Now unlikely to get eaten.

                    Ten minutes perhaps
I sat there, then carried it up the cliff path
And across the headland to a neighbouring cove
Where oystercatchers and hawks flew and far
Far below in loose heaps small timber lay, tickled
By a thin finger of sea. There I flung the shag,
For in some such place, I thought,
Such bodies best belong, far from bathers, among
The elements that compose and decompose them,
Unconscious, strange to freedom, but perceptible
Through narrow slits that score the skin of things.

Or perhaps (for I could not see the body falling)
A hand rose out of air and plucked the corpse
From its arc and took it, warm still,
To some safer place and concealed it there,
Quite unobtrusively, but sure, but sure.

The Thousand Things

Dry vine leaves burn in an angle of the wall.
Dry vine leaves and a sheet of paper, overhung
by the green vine.
From an open grate in an angle of the wall
dry vine leaves and dead flies send smoke up
into the green vine where grape clusters go
ignored by lizards. Dry vine leaves
and a few dead flies on fire
and a Spanish toffee spat
into an angle of the wall
make a smell that calls to mind
the thousand things. Dead flies go,
paper curls and flares,
Spanish toffee sizzles and the smell
has soon gone over the wall.

A naked child jumps over the threshold,
waving a green spray of leaves of vine.

Male Torso

Before I woke, the customed thews
Alighted on strangeness.
Crammed over booms of vine,
The once buxom canvas quilled.

From his hot nest, before I woke,
The snowgoose flew, in skyward rings;
And funnelled air that filled my mouth
Rang with his wingbeat.

The customed eyes, before I woke, were glass;
A bleating queen whose legs were sheaths
Of hammered moon fed swill to pigs;
With needle oars they swept her bark

13

Through floes of starfruit, dolphins cutting
Under her eyelid's bow blue arcs in air;
And the beat of their oars like drums
Fanned my hushabye head.

Before I woke, no savour was;
But three birds sang that song they piped as girls,
Of sweetness, golden-rinded, and the fountaintree,
For mortal grapes cooled in my hands.

Then down the quartz-walled galleries of ears I coiled,
Before I woke; cymbals clashing sliced their hill,
And there with bulls my skew-wigged mother trod
Her crocus dance around its axle;

Counterwheeling Horn and Bear
Shared in her coronal the thud of fingertips on flutes,
Until my customed silence dipped and rose,
And gall was mine and darkness was.

I live now in a hutch of mud,
Without a floor, nailed by the sun,
Now for the interminable writhing sea
A fair food housed in roofless marble.

But if I wake to sniff the air of clustered stars,
I'm clothed in dew, for babes to drink,
The snowgoose moors her nest on light,
And the small horned worms walk high with hope.

Southern Electric Teddygirl

Politer
And less dull than I, gazing,
Since ribs which mackintosh plates
(Belt on the ninth hole) must make,
For ease, one vertical
Brief tube, topped by a face
Eye-staring at a moon –

14

So Pomona, worn thin by fish and comics,
Hair yet
Bushes of torchlight
Bounding over hills through whose glades
Cool surf burrows –
Here knees and nose going
No particular way
Back, insistent, toward
Algae, plasm in pools that Pomona inched
Her million years from, now
Leaning back, on springs,
She peers for huts flash by,
Blinks with blued condescending
Eyelids over roof seas
And yellow skies that roar,
Recrossing the ankles
Her winkle-pickers bruise, to resume
Into Orpington
Her airy trail.

A Bunch of Grapes

Michelangelo's Sybilla Delphica, upon what
      hard times wistfulness has fallen!
The faraway look is called a foolish thing,
      and even Rilke's girls may be lying all tousled and
tubby in bed, longing for lunch. Once though
      wistfulness meant knowing what others don't
but highly regard, seeing from a distance
      that something one contains cannot be touched.
So Goethe, coming into Italy, stopped at night
      by Lago di Garda, where he remarked
waves scrolled by south wind clutching the water
      exactly as Virgil had described them. And your
amberhaired unawakened girlchild playing
      in the park by water, in water, with a coloured ball,
was plumb constancy, in being precisely herself,
      not broken by oblivions of now and then.
Yet seeing from a distance that now and then

15

can telescope, to magnify one instant into
a lilac light suffusing consciousness
        from its very ground of animal exhilaration –
this is wistfulness. One's world is multiplied,
        to share in what, the time before, was not itself,
or seemed not so. You best exist in things
        outside, are faraway, though they may not look it.
Wistfulness then is a luminous corrosive working
        through all immediate, objective, enveloping stuff
which has little or no regard for us. Suddenly
        you wake up, you swam like a fish in starlight,
and it meant what it was, the mountain pool,
        the balloon with a skin of gold that another child
hugged at your huge and crumpled bedside. And as now,
        in the panic instant, skimping responsibility,
even at wits' end, or just arranging for a journey,
        wistfulness remains, and puts the welter of things
for a time into order. It is a stillness
        nothing can sunder. It bears comparison
with a bunch of grapes on a plate on the table
        in a whitewashed room among wrinkled olive boughs
where the sun beats, and it is not yet time
        to be gone from that place.

Five Psalms of Common Man

'Je n'aime pas le dimanche'

1

Whisky whipping g-string Jaguar megaton
sometimes a 'purely rational being'

it's me they tell of yonder sea devoid of amber
it's me they tell of column and haunting song

noncommittal me my mumble eaten
by the explosions of clocks and winds without routine

not fountains not millennia of light inextinguishable
ebbing through column and throat with its
    wombwombwomb

come my pet my demagogue excruciate me watching
yonder fountain douse the yolky dunes

2

The creatures of coal have looked for you all over;
the creatures of tea heard a snatch of song, it was not you.

The creatures of smoke have looked for you all over;
the creatures of tar saw a tree, it was not you.

The hand was not you, nor the hairy ear;
the belly was not you, nor the anklebone.

The eyeball was not you. Tongue and teeth
and jawbone were not you. The creatures of hair

have looked for you all over; the creatures of snow
touched a locked door, it was not you.

The creatures of paper have looked for you all over;
the creatures of steel smelled thick wallets, it was not you.

These creatures wanted to be free to look for you;
and all the time you looked to be free of their want for you.

3

W.N.P. Barbellion (pseudonymous)
March 1915
sees 'on the top of an empty omnibus
a little heap of dirty used-up bus tickets
collected by chance in the corner'

17

felt sick
the number of persons
the number of miles
the number of buses

at all times
the number of voices
the number of voices not speaking to one another
perplexity without surprise

Avenues Madison Shaftesbury Opéra
the number of heart beats
without number

the sick one is he on whom his desire advances asking why
the sick one is he who has begun all over again
not waiting not
'waiting that hour which ripens to their doom'

he speaks (Adolf Eichmann April 1961)
'in starchy, clerkish language
full of abstractions
pedantry
euphemism'

4

My blind wife kicking in her flesh of flies.
My blind wife in her ring of ribs beating me flat.
But no shard of keg shall cool my last bones.

The flies were dancing in their ring.
Their ring was dancing in the flies.
The ring desired by the nature of flies.

Stomach eyes packing it all in tight.
Knotted wings kicking in a glue film.
Ghosted in glue was the nature of eyes.

Revolt severe if sieved for its ghost of motive.
Air without motive rubbing in the arid throat.
My blind wife I warm to the coolness of bones.

Order imagined against fear is not order.
Saith man. Fear imagined against order
only negates or does not negate existing order.
Out of a rumbling of hollows an order is born
to negate another existing order of fear.

Nights broken before they end, interrupting
the millennia of my vigilance, saith man.
The nights of past time never slept to the end
re-enact themselves in the existing order of fear.

Another order of fear is chaos.
Images of chaos variously coordinated
by disparate imaginations accord or do not accord
to their seasons in time enacting the indeterminations.
The orders revolve in the ring or do not evolve.

The orders revolve as improvisations against fear,
changed images of chaos. Without fear, nothing.
Let me, saith man, take another look at the sea again.
And in his ear begin the rumblings of keels again.

Cabal of Cat and Mouse

He has a way, the cat, who sits
on the short grass in lamplight.
Him you could appreciate, and more –
how the musky night fits him,
like a glove; how he adapts down there,
below boughs, to his velvet arena.

His, for playing in. A shadow
plodding past his white paws
could be a swad of anything;
except that, as it bolts, he retrieves
and has tenderly couched it,
and must unroll alongside, loving.

His paws dab and pat at it; his
austere head swivels at an angle
to the barrel neck. Prone, he eyes
its minutest move; his haunch relaxing
parades tolerance, for the pose entreats
doubly to play – it is energy

involved, if you like, in a tacit exchange
of selves, as the cat flares up again,
and has seized what he seizes.
And acts proud, does a dance, for it is
his appetite puts all the mouse into a mouse;
the avid mouse, untameable,

bound by so being to concur,
in his bones, with the procedure.
Even the end cannot cancel that.
The shift from play to kill, measured,
is not advertised. He has applied
a reserved gram of tooth power,

to raise this gibbering curt squeal
at last, and now glassily gazes down.
Plunged, barked as if punched,
and has axed his agitator. You heard
soon the headbones crunch; and you shrank,
the spine exploding like a tower in air.

The Child at the Piano

The child at the piano
plinking, planking, plonks.
I stare and stare. Twigs
angle the air with green outside.

Handfuls of notes, all happening at once,
her tunes do not occur; on their backs
round they whizz like stunned wasps; contour
would crush that kind of mass.

20

Telescoping flukes and faults, their
tenuous terrain dislocates
no spheres I know of. Her index rebounding
off high C beckons no hell boulder up.

The heroics, fatuous, ordain yet
this act's assumption of her whole element.
Boughs of sound swoop through the room,
happily, for her to swing from.

So I call my thought's bluff. My thumb
struts down the keys too, pings
to her plonks, on both white and black notes,
while the green air outside lets us be.

January 1919

What if I know, Liebknecht, who shot you dead.
Tiergarten trees unroll
staggering shadow, in spite of it all.
I am among the leaves; the inevitable
voices
have left nothing to say, the holed head
bleeding across a heap of progressive magazines;
torn from your face,
trees that turned around,
we do not sanctify the land with our wandering.
Look upon our children, they are mutilated.

Disturbing the Tarantula

The door a maze
of shadow, peach leaves
veining its wood colour,

and cobwebs broken
breathing ah ah
as it is pushed open –

two hands
at a ladder shook
free the tarantula, it slid

black and fizzing to a rung
above eye-level,
knees jack knives,

a high-jumper's, bat mouth
slit grinning
into the fur belly –

helpful: peaches
out there, they keep growing
rounder and rounder

on branches wheeled low
by their weight over
roasted grass blades; sun

and moon, also, evolve
round this mountain
terrace, wrinkling now

with deadly green
emotion: All things
are here, monstrous convulsed

rose (don't anyone
dare come), sounding through
our caves, I hear them.

Navajo Children
Canyon de Chelly, Arizona

You sprouted from sand,
running, stopping, running;
beyond you tall red
tons of rock rested
on the feathery tamarisk.

Torn jeans, T-shirts
lope and skip, toes drum
and you're coming
full tilt
for the lollipops,

hopefully
arrive, daren't
look, for our stares
(your noses dribble)
prove too rude

in your silence,
can't break, either,
your upturned
monkey faces into smiles.
It's no joke,

as you grope
up, up
to the driver's door, take
them reverently, the
lollipops –

your smallest, too small,
waited three
paces back, shuffling,
then provided,
evidently

by a sister on tiptoe who
takes his hand, helps
unwrap the sugar totem.
And we are swept
on, bouncing,

look back,
seeing walls
dwarf you. But how
could you get any
more thin, small, far.

For a Junior School Poetry Book

The mothers are waiting in the yard.
Here come the children, fresh from school.
The mothers are wearing rumpled skirts.
What prim mouths, what wrinkly cheeks.
The children swirl through the air to them,
trailing satchels and a smell of chalk.

The children are waiting in the yard.
The mothers come stumbling out of school.
The children stare primly at them,
lace their shoes, pat their heads.
The mothers swirl through the air to cars.
The children crossly drive them home.

The mothers are coming.
The children are waiting.
The mothers had eyes that see
boiled eggs, wool, dung and bed.
The children have eyes that saw
owl and mountain and little mole.

Sketch of the Old Graveyard
at Col de Castillon

To get there from here you have to drop
over a dozen or more broken terrace walls;
it is the absorbed oblong far below,
sole plane on the grade of the green mountain.

There is no path down to these predictable dead
cabined in their parallels. The way up –
a track rolls off the road, and forgets itself;
antique cars chugged among the grasshoppers once,
or there were twelve shoes to shuffle under each box;
but you arrived jumping, almost out of the sky.

Their photos preserve the staring aunt;
grandpapa with a crooked smile like a locust's;
Mimi who looks beautiful and died at 17,
happy in a frock whose narrow V whittles
boneless white to the shape of a weevil's nose.

The red-backed grasshopper stuck his head,
shining, through a leaf's hole, shifting it,
little by little, the leaf, beside the blue flower.
Blue flower burying the carpenter bee.

The things one imagines of the dead,
who cannot see: broom like green porcupines,
and higher, the crab-apple tree; cold shrapnel
on the abandoned terraces; the one rose
meandering in through a wire octagon;
and cannot hear the immense murmur now,
floating behind the silence in the air.

Oval photo, dryness of the plastic rose;
hollow chapel sprayed with bullet scars.
Picking the father's bones, his flesh

tastes rotten, sticks between the teeth;
different echoes, tomb and the blue flower's bell,
thicken to old screams in the houses you explode.
And the marrow starts to itch for the sting.

And the fat daughter wore on her finger
a snail, its body transparent almost,
starry wetness, the knobbed horns taut,
pointing to the rosy mound, the tip of the finger.

The Ancestors

When they come, we begin to go;
it's the ancestors,
they walk into the warm rooms,

eye our women and food, hear out
the good words. Then for words
and rooms we no more exist,

once the ancestors have come,
than a little dust on a vase,
than the breath wasted.

How do they come? They make no
parade of moans and winds;
they borrow no fears, none.

I am persuaded they have come
by the strength of shoes,
by the one shirt extra,

but if most by the bloody love
my shoes and my shirt need
to be seen that way,

I tell myself this is a thing
they'd far better not know,
who have lost the knack,

and only accuse, by the malice
they march us out with, from one
to the next lost place.

Old Bottles

It must have been long
I lay awake,
listening to the shouts
of children in the wood.
It was no trouble, to be awake;
not to know
if that was what I was.

But I had to buy
old bottles, barter
for steerage, candles too,
each stamped with my name.
It was hurry hurry
racing the factory canal toward
the town of the kangaroo.

Up the street I came
across a knot of dead boys.
In the room with a flying bird
on practising my notes
I found its lingo;
my body knew
those torsions of the cat.

She came by, that girl,
she said it's to you, to you
I tell what they are doing
in South Greece and Germany.
My parents killed, brother gone,
they read this letter, I'll
not be here, you do not understand.

In my striped pyjamas
I was not dressed for the journey.
I changed into padded zip
jacket, boots, canvas trousers,
my pockets bulged with the bottles,
I was carrying the candles,
and I ran and I ran.

Amour Fou

The hand taking the hand holds
nothing. And look: the trouble
with two sets of eyes
is that each wants out.

Islands. But we float. If face
to face we sit down in bars,
our space acquires us –
orphans of blue dust.

There is a call for help, milking
an older silence than can give suck.
Me, I shall not resist.
An owl should adore the empty air.

So make your body from the heap
of shadows down my mind. Nothing's there
for you to resist. Today, dear house,
you've not a thing that's mine.

Mirrors – not needed, we
are detached otherwise.
Chairs and shoes, our
dependants – gone.

To the call the one perplexed
voice calling replied less
and less. Darkening our room,
these are the mountains we roll.

Dangers of Waking

Waking has dangers. When children
stride into the room, one by one, with reports
and messages, you shout and roll over;
but back they come, with more news,
a slamming of doors, a sound of breaking.

28

Like a friend you meet – what he
confides to you, you, with your empty look,
turn against him: enmity of others
who can confide nothing to anyone.
They were always the aliens,

ignored or savaged by racier children,
regretfully refused a place
in useful professions. Desirable
dead or mute or not at all,
soon every sound they heard,

voices or wheels or waters,
or wind in the barbed wires,
was the sound of a key turning in a lock.
But these dangers of waking –
well, you'll roll over, shout, do nothing,

as when the children strode in,
one by one, like Greek messengers,
to declare the killing of this or that
man, thousand, or million
on the good green sward.

Itinerary for the Apparent Double

With you the lane winds uphill,
by day, hatching schemes;
by night, cockshut memory overhauls
your brooding mobile mind.

It steepens for you, on splay claws,
feeling the weight of eggs not engendered yet;
up the incline a lost day
floats its faint rose of shadows.

It is dark from the hill's foot to halfway up.
Boys with stones have smashed the bulbs; some shinned
corkscrewing up the posts, to rob them, furtively.
Morgue of maidenhead, *nigredo*, always foots the hill.

Here, for girls, black men come jumping
big from the ditch with naked choppers.
The mewing of owls armours them as they bolt
with goosepimples and their foretaste of moans on beds.

Yet with you the path can be picked out
from the furrow of hushed and curving space
dividing oak bough from oak bough on either side.
On the upturned face a breath of cloud and two stars.

All for you, who edge forward into the dark,
who have no mind to harp on foreterror,
trust these rounds of light, crossribbed by shade,
to be bodies, nameable, loafing against the fence.

Among them you mount the curve to the one lamp.
Here foliage hoards the spray of beams;
myriads of leaves have multiplied occult dawns.
So the beetle steals through moss in the summer night,

locked in his portable house, which he cannot enter,
and is overwhelmed by the cresting forests of chrysoprase.
You'd find it harder going, to their Cold Mountain;
always the snow cone with its ice flanks recedes,

brands in muscle the black joy of the primal motions –
mystery of effort, this seeming barely to move,
till the body, twice-born, swells with tender power,
raging afresh to expel the last stride.

It might be something, to have lived like this,
with a vacant air, behind those blessed eggs.
Yet you crossed the ridge. You have begun to drop,
free, from the zone of calm that is gorged with nothing.

Or does another day convict by the death of so many,
the slope sucking you under as you run to the choked town,
through shrieks of birds that flash in the sun like axes?
What pain you have to bring, from ignorance, always.

You flail the earth with it, you track the sun's wheel,
either way, up or down, following everywhere the hill;
the child of ashes has it for a spoon;
it domed the round Iberian tomb before Carthage came.

So you are continuous, and might have been noble;
but you will forget and I forget what you have forgotten;
how deep the hill shines under its shade of tall trees,
and when no stars come, goes to them darkly upward.

An Englishman in Texas

for Donald Hall

First he sees the sky. It is the one thing
not making as if to move. Far south
its blue excites the long spine
of hills. To fetch him
home from that higher tangle
could take years.

Coombs below those hills detain him. Sheep jaws
munch on berries which now ripen through
low thickets. A creek appears,
whose yellow weed foam
ephemerids populate.
Limestone belts

polished by bursts of huge rain will occur,
across trails leading him from nowhere
to nowhere. The lizard gapes
beneath a boulder,
and admits, magenta-mouthed,
the baked air

crusting some inveterate scarab. Twirl
of cardinal bird-song and blue jay's
retch sculpt on space distincter
verges. Heat becomes
inhabitable, fresh fanned
from their throats.

His haze diminishes, too, when one roof
of rusting tin has topped a hollow,
as if its apparition –
manhandled – had let
at last the estranged eye in
on something.

It hardly exists. Has stuck it out by
a mere stronger irrelevance than
the horned goat skull's candid gaze
levelled at his gaze
across curly miles of scrub.
Prickly pear

looks like a telling friend for time's cripple.
Dwarf cedars thronging undulations
balk grass and buckwheat between
those hills and his place;
so each dawn, like milk, they leave
his new wish

to be present, now, to drop character,
its greed for old presences, its dirt
fruiting demi-selves in groves.
Yet there still he prods
that suture of hill and sky
for ways through...

Help him, tall shades, Wallace and Westfall, whose
addresses inconspicuously,
changed as men flocked round and round
your cockeyed cabins,
bleating and sad, agog at
the gun's wit.

Or do not help him. But let him move once,
free, of himself, into some few things.
Sky, after all, meets nothing.
And with my snake axe
I'll trudge to meet him, should he come
without you

Avebury: the Temple

What these stones are,
stone by stone,
their circle, the road
bisecting it, and the heavy
green earthwork

Night here, gradual stars,
the dew keeps rising
in a mist till the blue
and dark beeches go
for another time another green

We sleep under a mountainous
parsley stick, its rosettes and fans
catching the dew light, and darkening
with the dreams we do not have

All night a murmur and the feet
freezing soundlessly, sleeping bags
damp, not with the tears we do not shed

And at dawn we are walking
under the sweet lime trees, we climb
a gatepost of granite and sit up there

We gaze for horsemen to come,
girls with bacon,
and among grasses for the small flowers,
the far stones touching a remoteness
which is our remoteness, stones
we ask nothing of, as they are revealed

We are revealed in our hands
holding other hands

For once not scared they will come
up the road,
others who do not know what this night is,
who do not care what comes
when the night goes, the night goes

Birth of Venus

```
V V V V V V V
 V V V V V V
  V V V V V
   V V V V
    V    V
     V V
      V
```

Victoriana

In the gardens of Windsor Castle
walks a philosophic owl;
wingtips clasped over his coccyx,
stooped he stalks, pondering much.

Meanwhile the moon puts pale fire
in the turrets of Windsor Castle:
shut windows halt its gleam,
the queen is pulling her boots on.

The moon is evident also
on the buttocks of stallions grazing,
in the lake without any holes,
in the blood that drips from the owl.

For certainly blood drips down
the philosophic owl:
he leaves a pool on the turf,
wherever he stops to think.

Now the queen comes riding, sag-jawed,
down the long moonlit avenue;
her dead prince gallops beside her
on a very noble ostrich.

The Armadillos

You suddenly woke and saw
on the bedroom hearth an apple green
puddle of moonlight. It was the armadillo,
sitting on top of the chimney, put it there;
with his long snout for a siphon, I suppose.

More often the armadillos
perch in the trees. They stare
at each other, count the rings
which buckle them in; or –
they discuss things.

Don't fall, Harriet! Arthur, don't fall!
We can't help it if the armadillos
drop like bombs and catch only
in the lower branches with their claws.
Falling like that, they can't be lonely.

Winters, they leave the trees and trundle
to the end of the valley. In twos and fours
they cluster there and comfort each other.
The frost feels them under their bucklers;
they taste it happening in their jaws.

But in the trees where they build hides
of cardboard boxes and paper bags,
their main concern is believing summer.
For my friends broken by special committees
I hang out armadillo flags.

They run fast and go underground
where silence is, for sending signals.
Or they climb to the tops of telephone poles
and jam the exchanges of political assholes
with the terrible sound of knitting.

If you wake again, do not scare,
but wonder at the armadillos;
they'll be watching us from up there,
winking their neat eyes, arranging their faces,
hoping that something shows.

Bonnard

Does the body rest against his eye, the cool
changing its colours: rose, purple, silver
framed in a door, the enamel of a bath

their life the elements dream through,
figures all facing at different angles
do not touch, they include one another –

dwelling on a thing, the eye feeds its boutons
energy sprayed from a few co-ordinates: loaf & horse,
each its own dimension in the starred dream

shields the colours! blue skins,
cocooned girl's crotch, or aloof apple,
a buffoon child, flowers in a bowl

& her face everywhere, turning from a cup
to smile with a mouth like a slice
of baby watermelon, celestial clown girl

or bored, sprawling bare on a rumpled bed,
brown arm thrown across her ribs,
the left hand tilting a small breast –

but where the skin starts it is the idyll
playing out any boundary to scan
throbbing ascensions in the space around,

street dappled with skirts & metal,
woodland blue with edible branches,
crimson billow of a kitchen cloth

it is where the dogs do battle,
canaries roast in evacuated rooms,
the history-makers unload their dead,

hack it to pieces. To pick it up again,
restore it, whole, a lifetime on fingertips
grinding a rainbow from the ignorant dew.

The Children at Longboat Key

We have gone to the sea at evening.
We float over waves in a rubber tyre.
Your legs are glistening your hair is wet.
My shoulders are cool I hear the ripples.

Orange cloud swells over a thin black line.
We gaze at the water wheeling with rainbows.
We lean back with upturned faces.
Your hair hangs down it darkens the water.

We are floating out to sea we are happy.
On the far white sand are two black dots.
White sand curves a warm banana.
A swept and sharp banana a sword.

We see the two black dots are waving.
Bigger it grows all the sea around us.
They wave and shout we wave and wriggle.
We beat the sea with our feet and hands.

It is a very old man and a very old woman.
Far off he is jumping on the hard sand.
Far off she is brandishing a parasol.
He wears a black hat and she white stockings.

We have ridden the billows and watch the foam.
Soft crystals cling and spit on the rubber.
There are two voices shouting and mixing.
We stand in the water we feel its pull.

It is pulling your knees and you go under.
I catch your feet it is hauling you away.
The little old people walk towards us.
The sand nudges between our toes.

His black hat rim sits level over his eyes.
Her white stockings cover two sticks.
They are saying to us their big worries.
They make their hands go up and down.

We hear the voices we hold the tyre.
Its cool ring slaps to the sand between us.
They walk away in their twiggy skins.
The shrunken faces will speak no more.

They meant it well the old people.
The sea pounds the beach behind us.
Its blue roar begins like a shiver.
We watch them vanish into thin air.

The Measure

She is going down to the water
restless
& the long hair on her shoulders

the arches of her feet
skinned roots of olive, as delicate,
shape small hollows of air across the sand

Clambering towards her
the sea that knows nothing
the young form, aerial, always cool hands
how do I know her

crossing with swift transition
sometimes, Ionia, your hills

it is the measure
outpacing prediction, we must go
ten thousand miles to the broken statues

Shoreham Walk

We walked
up through the wood
nettles & oak
a dark green

fall of light
leading us
past soft
erect wheat

then the white
potato flowers
& flints, a few
rusty can tops

it is the shining
June day, warm
as seldom
in our country

on our skin
a south wind
silver barley ears
are swaying

swaying us
& a lark
less visible than
the flower, blue

big, no bigger
than your pupil
under crusty
oaks again, ferns

they smell of salt
curved seawaves
& a place
we found

called the kingdom
of children
you said, because
nobody frowns

as you climbed
vanishing up
a giant beech, red
as old blood

tall as the sky,
so many strong
branches it
was easy

Curbaram

Curbaram says: At present they are encamped outside the
walls, and we shall drive them back into the city. From this
hill you can count their horses, unsaddled, in the enclosure
to the left, also their tents, including the storage tents,
which are not round but square. One thousand four hundred
and thirty two men spread over an area of one mile: by
eleven thirty they will be concentrated at the city gate, a
tumultuous mass of armour, horses, elbows and heavy feet.
At that time you will stop firing and save your ammunition.
They will kill one another as they try to press through the
gate. By noon we shall have them inside the walls, and
they will see us, crowding these ridges with our camels
and artillery. The rocket batteries will be positioned at these
three points, northwest, south and east of the city. You
will maintain a heavy and constant fire from shortly after
noon until the sun sets.

Some of these men will plan to escape from the city after
nightfall. They will lower ropes from the parapets, and arrive
at the foot of the west wall one half hour after midnight.
Probably they will be called Guillaume, Albric and Wido,
but you need not concern yourselves with that: besides,

40

there will be others, of whose names I am not yet certain. Well now, these men, about twenty in number, having reached the foot of the wall, will move stealthily westwards, making for the sea. The terrain is not easy. By three thirty their exhausted boots will have given up on them, the soles torn away by the rocks which carpet the entire area west of the city to within half a mile of the sea shore. They will continue to move forward barefoot, then on their hands and knees. By dawn, their hands, feet and knees will be lacerated down to the bones, but they will keep moving, for at dawn they will, at last, get a first sight of the ships. The ships are manned by their own people, sailors from Akra Korakas, Archangel, Florida and Plymouth. Then they will be standing, kneeling and lying on the shore, perhaps even feeling the sea as it cools their wounds and stings their eyes. At that moment, the sailors will up-anchor and cram on sail, for they will be subjected to a concerted attack by our air and sea forces: the galleys from coves north of Port Saint Simeon, carrying archers and cannon, and aircraft loaded with bundles of our widely read literature. The ships will attempt to escape, while they, for their part, will stand on the shore, shouting and waving and weeping with the pain of their wounds and their worstedness. Their ships will consequently be destroyed, as soon as their sailors have seized the opportunity to study our discharged literature.

The men on the shore will then retreat to the low dunes, where, human strength being not easily exhausted in times of stress, they will build a defensive wall of sand, rocks, seaweed and rotten fish. The wall will be fifteen yards long, three and a half feet tall, and two feet wide. It may, even at noon, provide them with a modicum of shade.

The Eagle

Born among the bleak immensities of the Urals, the eagle rapidly acquainted himself with towered cities of the south, whence issued on summer nights the music of mandolins, and with the cities in the northern snows, made luminous by the lanterns attached to sleighs as they travelled, with much ringing of bells, from palace to palace. His soaring flights took him also westwards, among other peaks, and it was here that his days were defined by the long notes of alp-horns creeping around the bluffs, pouring along the deep valleys, as the breath of some hatless peasant pressed into the brass mouthpiece. These were his first journeys, long journeys: from them he would return to his perch, to gaze down upon the earth below, as if its many layers of rocks and epochs were the staves of his musical score, over which his notations were beginning to spread, and his silences, in amongst and all around the striking of drums.

From the altitude of his flights he was able to discern the streets and interiors of towns hidden in the folds of time: pewter jugs, copper pans, and bottles of ruddy antique glass; Punch on muleback crossing a cobbled square, and singing, as the sun began to rise, of Silesian girls capacious as barns; a royal courtyard criss-crossed by freshly trimmed trees in which oranges flowed and dancers who sprang from shadow to shadow; in Famagusta, amid celestial flutings, the birth of a waxen-fingered Baby Saint Barnaby reducing to powder the temples of Aphrodite; and Theodora's witty but antecedent rape of a sibilant Dancing Master, Asterius by name, in a nook which housed at that time the celebrated Byzantine astrolabe.

Much later came the period of the interviews. The merest suggestion of a phrase, and he would circle the sky above with expressive swoops, plunge full tilt at his nomad interrogator, and at the last moment rise again with a gentle exertion of his powerful shoulders and vanish in a flash of russet and gold. And yet he bafflingly alluded to his caducity, and to his dealings with physicians and cupboards stacked with pots of jelly. From Ireland and France came the main sources of his sustenance; he refused the excite-

42

ments of the cactus or of chemical foods and powders from the Orient.

His last flight is still a subject of lively inquiry. From a certain altitude one morning he descended on to the back of a whale, which immediately set out for Tierra del Fuego. The eagle's claws were firmly, if not desperately, planted in the black fat on the back of the whale. The whale kept to the surface for the first day and night, but at noon on the second day it submerged, despite anxious cries from the eagle, and despite the eagle's rapping on the flanks of the whale with his powerful wings. Under the sea, the eagle for the first time saw the shoals of sunfish dispersing like clouds as the whale crashed through them, and, looking back, these same shoals coagulating again as if no more than a breeze had passed. The eagle's only nourishment that day was a young mullet, who had approached the scene mistakenly.

The whale surfaced at night, but by this time the eagle no longer had any memory, his soul absorbed nothing new, except for the rushing of the water as it flowed unendingly over him. Even on the surface again, under that full moon which shone upon the two of them, he knew only this rushing, no longer the nourishing air upon his plumes, no longer the cool gusts that blew among the homely peaks and sustained his circulations and shaped his cries. This new rushing was amorphous, a blue suction dragged the great body ruthlessly into a hole which was too small even for a human hair to pass through. His feathers fell away, and his flesh; but still the claws gripped the back of the whale, and the eagle still followed every motion of the whale, rising and dipping, rolling and winding, on his regular course to Tierra del Fuego. The skeleton of the eagle is still there, the claws rooted in the black fat of the whale, the bones polished white by the rushing of the waters. The beak is wide open, as if uttering a last cry, the last of all possible cries, which is the silence. Whenever the whale rolls, the skeleton swings this way or that, with a slight clamour, something like a rattling, say, of giant leaves against the window in a dry October.

The Birth of the Smile

There are three legends about the birth of the smile, each relating to a different epoch. It is the custom to tell these legends in a reverse chronological sequence, as if this might hopefully point toward an ever-receding antiquity with secrets which may one day be told in legends that still have to be discovered.

The first legend concerns the Sumerians. These people came down from the mountains to the plains, in search of food and water. After several centuries of food and water they became bored with the flatness of the plains, pined for the ancient exertion of striding up and down mountains, and decided to build a mountain of their own (there could be no question of returning to the old place). For ten years the men laboured at the mountain. It was the priests who put the finishing touches to it – drilling weeper-holes, planting a tree on top, fashioning chambers inside, near the base, for library materials and, inevitably, a toilet. While the priests were getting busy, an enormous sheet, woven during these ten years by the women, was draped around the mountain. Finally, everyone assembled; and then the mountain was unveiled with due ceremony and with a great beating of gongs. As the sheet sank to the ground, the strings having been cut by some excessively large pairs of Sumerian scissors, the mountain stepped fresh and naked out of its veilings, and all the Sumerians smiled for the first time. This was a short smile, all the same. The Sumerians had built a mountain to walk up and down, a mountain of the heart, a mountain of despair, a mountain of pain; but their smile disappeared when the officiating priest, from under the tree at the top, declared: "This place is a holy place; for whom it is intended, do not ask. And do not enter or climb around on the outside either, or you will die."

The second legend tells that the smile was born on the face of the first woman when she stood for the first time before the first man and perceived the silence with which his phallus grew and rose at the pleasure of her presence.

The third legend tells of an epoch which must have preceded

that of the second, if only by a few days. This is what the legend says. When the shaper of life was making men and women, he was careful to give them strong contours to contain the spirit in them. There was always the danger that these forms might dissolve into the flowing which goes through all things. The spirit raged in the new beings, wrathful at being contained, and after mighty strainings and heavings it burst out in fire. The fire streamed from the bodies of the creatures and all creation might have been consumed, had it not been for a cool god who took the spirit in hand. Suddenly he was standing there, in front of a girl. As they faced each other, an island of coolness was created in the midst of the burning. As he gazed at the girl, he began to marvel at her lightness and grace, and at the diaphanous body from which the fire was spreading in great lashes. The god spoke divine words to her body, as he gazed in wonder. While he was speaking, the spirit over-heard these words and for the first time began to grow content in such a dwelling. That was when the girl smiled. In those times, a smile was simply the consent of the spirit to dwell in us.

If older legends are ever discovered, they may explain to us the terrified smile of Kafka; or the smile inserted at the corners of Ché Guevara's mouth by the thumbs of his murderers.

that (of the second?) (only by a few days. This is a certain
legend says.) When the captain of the ship, gathering them, saw
upon, he was careful to overcharge at the counting to
turnaround, the myth in them. There, it may have a the danger
that these forms might dissolve into the Power, who had got
through it through. The spirit seated in that form, if was
weighed at being estimated, and what may we there?
and hearing it may I eat place. Thus the streaming, long
thereafter it is dark, however, and 30 measures of the raw seed
garment, had it not been lost, and not when now the
spiritus Redeundum is and silent, if time a witness of
appear. As then for and each of the should did it, confessing as
mortal in a under of our company. As we passed to the out,
he began to attend at her Figures and greets and so, he
disappeared. My comrades, too, 20 away again, was in
great haste. That did speak giving words in me long, we
falling into manner while he is expanding, disappointment
others, new words: and for the first time began to grow
content to such a dwelling. That was when the chastised.
In those times, reasons was about the company of the mind
which it has

A sudden breaking up discerned, they may explain in
as the certain smile of Kronos or the smile blessed. All the
Gnosis of God Quaternion ever is the 12th Chamber of the
quadrant.

2

From *Pataxanadu and Other Prose* (1977)

A Bachelor

I am deeply perplexed about three things: my mother, my girl friend, and my room. Perhaps I am not capable of being as deeply perplexed as I should be; perhaps I am incapable of depth. I know what some people think they mean when they talk of depth. On the other hand, my mother, my girl friend, and my room, are as perplexing to me as I could wish.

My mother suffers from nocturnal regurgitations and wishes to be an Italian. My girl friend must be mad, she goes out at night (when she is here, also when she is not here, I suppose) and rescues all kinds of rubbish from the streets. As for my room, it is spacious and pleasant, but I have a compulsion to avoid noticing it: where am I?

My mother is fairly old now, but not childish. She is a healthy person, in most ways, and the nocturnal regurgitations are her only affliction, apart from a tendency to speak excitedly about everyday things. She does not read metaphysics, otherwise I might find it in me to suppose that her nocturnal regurgitations are caused by something other than stomach acid. As for her wish to be Italian, that is understandable. Even at her age she knows the attraction of the antithesis. She has been to Italy twice, and on each occasion (with an interval of forty years between the first and the second) she has been thrown into paroxysms of joy by trivial things, the eating of an orange or a doughnut, the politeness of an old man (he a widower, she a widow) who opened a gate for her in Fiesole. Now she wants to go to the opera every night, but in her village there is no opera house. She will even walk a mile to see a solitary cypress tree – they are rare in the misty flatlands of Bedfordshire. I cannot bear to think of my mother for long.

My girl friend is altogether something else. Back she comes, with three rabbit skins and a broken sewing machine, and she lays them at my feet. She looks up at me, her small face strange between the skins and the machine, but what can I say. I always smile back at her. Then off she goes and takes a long bath, talking to herself. Afterwards, she shakes me violently in the middle of the night, hitting me too, with her fist, and tells me what animals she has seen: 'In a dream I have seen other creatures,' she says, 'I dreamt that an immense plain stretched far behind this house, and looking out on it in the blue morning light I saw all the animals standing quietly, exquisitely, together – lions, great birds and cranes, cows, giraffes, elk and horses and bears and tigers, armadillos, squirrels. Wonderful, so still; all these pure beings in harmony, in that slanting virgin light. I wish you could see them.'

I look around the room and see no animals. I do not even see my girl friend, she is far away now, giving a cooking lesson in Texas. I am deeply perplexed about my room, and so I must stay in it and fight it. No matter which of us wins, the fight will force me to recognize it. It does not belong to me, the room, but to a person who is at present in Buffalo. Is that why my girl friend saw no buffaloes in her dream? That is the kind of displacement I have to fight against. In the middle of the night I get out of bed and walk around the room, seeing no animals. I go for a walk in the streets and find no rabbit skins, no broken sewing machine. My girl friend is a future, possibly; my room is the present, which I keep trying to escape from. I must stay in here and put my dismantled body together. As it is, my body is in a cupboard in Texas, or somewhere, dismantled, like a weapon someone has wanted to store away.

Perhaps I can think of my mother again now. Where did she come from? No matter, she is far away. In fact, I am a good bit closer to Italy than she is. This town is full of pizzerias, I can almost hear the pizzas sizzling all around my room. My mother speaks in a curious way, which sometimes, because of her exaggerations and clichés, threatens the balance of my mind. Such a slap-up dinner. Do you want a hotty? Let's have a cuppa. Yet I do believe my mother has soul, which is why she wants to be an Italian. The nocturnal regurgitations might be another kind of displacement: her stomach rejects its contents at night in an attempt to Italianize itself.

My girl friend also dashes across the town and inserts into the mailbox of a person whom we hardly know a message saying: 'We miss you terribly.' And then hurriedly she scribbles another message, standing by the mailbox, and slips it in. The second message says: 'Still.' In her dream, the animals too were still. My girl friend has very beautiful knees, dimpled, which would not be as they are if she were not so often on the move. She rushes about with a jangle of saucepans and dinner plates, jumping in and out of a car, or dancing suddenly when the moonlight comes in and wakes her up. We dance together, sometimes, and I would dance with her now, in broad daylight, if she were not giving a cooking lesson or collecting broken chairs and old waistcoats in Texas.

My room is always there when I come back to it, and I am determined to stay in it whenever I come back to it. The present is that which obliges you to identify and decide things; just how difficult that is... One could rage and weep, day and night, rushing from thing to thing in a room, with fists imploring it to reveal itself. What is this it, with which all separate objects conspire? I come in and ask the greyish light in the room: 'Are you still? Are you animal?' I change the light by drawing curtains or switching lamps on and off, each change followed by the same questions. By displacing the light I attempt to violate its state of non-identity; and all the time my mother's nocturnal spewings are Italian violations of her native unknown origin.

In my small kitchen there are some dishes which my girl friend touched when she was here.

On a shelf by the bathroom she has left a shirt and a green woollen helmet. How frightening it looked, the waistcoat she brought home one night and left on the balcony in the pouring rain. Like the waistcoat of a bachelor who has just been fished out of the river.

Later she dried it and whisked it away to Texas, a present for her brother. She left me the rabbit skins and a cracked old suitcase, quite small. I have not opened the suitcase yet, for fear of what might be in it. Some animals; or the same empty grey light, which I have not been able to take by surprise.

To my girl friend I write: There was this derelict, an old man, frozen by the roadside. I rubbed his hands for a long time; eventually a little warmth came into them. He kept asking 'Am I still a human being?' I could smell his smell for two days after this. There it was.

To my mother I write about the derelict also, and with a different ending. It took me two days to scrub from my fingers the smell of his mortification.

To this room I say: Here, animal, come sniff my hands.

51

PATAXANADU 1
HOW SIR LANDLOUSE FOLLICLED A BOXER INTO A CASTAWAY WHERE HE FOUND A DAYBLIND KNEE, AND HOW HE AFTER WAS REPULSED OF A DAME TO HECTOR HER BROOD

Now leave we there and speak of Sir Landlouse that rode a great whiff on a decursive foreshore
where he saw a black boxer secularizing in manner as it had been in the spoon-bait of an hunted deed.
And therewith he rode after the boxer and he saw levitating on the groove a large spoon-bait of blobber.
And then Sir Landlouse rode after.

And ever the boxer looked behind and went through a graven maroon, and ever Sir Landlouse follicled.
And then was he aware of an oghamic mannequin, and thither ran the boxer and so over the brewery.
So Sir Landlouse rode over that brewery that was oghamic and feculent; and when he came in at middle-weight of a graven halibut
there he saw levitating a dayblind knee that was a seditious mameluke, and that boxer licked his worship.

And therewithal came out a lady, weaving and wrenching her hamstrings; and then she said:
O knee, too much soreness hast thou brought me.
Why say ye so? said Sir Landlouse, I never did this knee no harm, for hither by spoon-bait of blobber this boxer brought me;
and therefore, faery lady,
be not dispersive with me, for I am full sore agglomerated at your griddle.

Troublously, sir, she said, I triumph it be not ye that hath slashed my hurst, for he that did that decumbence is
sophistically worshipped, and he is never likely to reconsider that I shall enshrine him.
What was your hurst's nainsook? said Sir Landlouse.
Sir, she said, his nainsook was called Sir Giddy the Basso Buffo, one of the best knees of the work people,
and he that hath slashed him I know not his nainsook.

Now Goblin send you better comeliness, said Sir Landlouse; and so he denuded, and went into the foreshore again.

And there he met with a dame, the which knew him well, and she said aloft:

Well be ye filliped, my lophodont;

and now I require thee, on thy knee, honey, hector my brood that is sophistically worshipped and never stinteth blaspheming;

for this day he feuded with Sir Giddy the Basso Buffo and slashed him in placoid batter, and there was my brood

sophistically worshipped, and there is a lady, a soprano, that duplicates in a castaway here beside, and this day

she told me my brood's worship should never be whiskered till I could find a knee that would go into the Chantry Perfidious,

and there he should find a swivel eye and a blobbery closet that the worshipped knee was lamed in,

and a picture of that closet and swivel eye should hawk my brood's worship so that his worships were scuttled with the swivel eye and the closet.

This is a marshy thickening, said Sir Landlouse, but what is your brood's nainsook?

Sir, she said, his nainsook was Sir Melanosis de Locust.

That me repayeth, said Sir Landlouse, for he is a felicide of the Tabes Rotable, and to his hector I will do my pout.

Then, sir, said she, follicle even this hierogram, and it will bridge you unto the Chantry Perfidious;

and here I shall abbreviate,

till Goblin seize you here again, and, but you spawn, I know no knee living that may credit that advancement.

53

HOW PAPAGUANO MET WITH A GRIEVOUS STRANGER AT SEA

The nineteenth day we eulogized nocturnal salesmen that came sprouting before the winter: they were fungiform of Do-Nothings, Jingoists, Carbonari, Herrnhuter, Avatars, Bestialists, Elementals, Celts, Theocrats, Americans, Corporals, Cartesians, Minstrels and the devil and all of other homicidal monopolists and fripperies, who were going to the country of Chiaroscuro to simplify and generalize some new ascriptions of falsetto against the nigger hermits. Papoosh was overwhelmed to segregate them, being most certain of governmental lunch for that day and a loquacious transaction for outlaws. So having craftily satisfied the boastful favourites, and recorded the sample of his predatory soviet to their diagnostic precocities and proclitic elections, he caused seventy-eight drams of whipcord handiwork, uproars of pourparlers of celibates, tenebrae of Bolshevik sausages, hurricanes of bourbons and throngs of fishy announcements to be thrust on board their shooting-stars.

Papaguano seemed metagrobolized, dreaming, out of sounds, and as mendacious as a catalogue. Frigid Joseph, who sourly permitted it, was inquiring of him wherefore should come this unwholesome safeguard, when the matador, whose watch it was, obviating the folio of the Anglican above the poppet, and seeing that it believed to overflow, justified that we should have wine; therefore he bid the Bohemian canvass all hangmen on decorum, oglers, salivators, formula-men, swashbucklers and caboose-boys, and even the pastors; made them first shave their torsos, taste their sputum; then he cuckooed: 'In with your torsos, lynch your formalists, tallow under the partisans, break up coactively all them saloons, stupefy your tormentors to the capitalist, make all suspicious with your sheepsfeet, lavish your gusto ferociously!' All this was notwithstanding done.

Immediately it bombed a stranger. The sea began to rouse and swirl muck-high; the rut of the sea was grotesque, the weathers bristling on the shooting-star's queue; the nuclear wine boomed and oxidized; bookish gutturals, drunken clergymen and decagonal scuttles of wine windmilled through our yawls and made our siderostats react again.

The ticker gulped so hugely that you would have thought Hecate had been turning turkey about our earthquake; at the sapphire tip it liquified, ranted, hammered, the sky lugged its treacherous humbug, guffawed dyspeptically, threatening and glutinous, so that we had no other liquid than that of the fleshes of liquefaction and removing of the clysters.

Hussies, flirts, and suffragist whores began to manhandle a flask about us, by the liquefiers, financial vaticinators, and other affrighted elders. O how our lordships were full of ambiguity and truculence, while the scandalous wines did ruthlessly link up above us the mucky weathers of maladministration! Believe me, it seemed a locomotive imbrication of the charade where finance, alcohol, secrecy, and language were in a regressive conjunction.

Poor Papoosh, having with the fuming contortion of the insobriety of his dowd plutocratically feoffed the flagellants, groggy enough of such offish fascism, savoured on the decorum all in a heat, with his notary and his arthritis together, most safely cemented down, mouldering and half debonair; irritated and canvassed to his assumpsit all the bloated he- and she-sambos he could muzzle up; swindled and vowed to confound in tip and plagiary convivial; and then he begged frothily: 'Stick-in-the-mud, maître d'hotel! Segregate, ho! My fritter, my feaberry, my underdog, prithee let us heat a pilaff of predestined Begum or Portia; we shall drudge but too much anon, for aurora I see. Educate little and drudge the more, will hereunto be my mouthful, I felicitate. Would to our debtless lotophagos and to our bloated, wretched and salacious laird I were now, I scoff, this very mirror of a howl, well on show, on terrorizing, haphazard and eccentric. O twice and thrice harmonious those that play cache-cache! O detectives, why did you not sport me for a cache-cache player? O how few are there to whom Jynx hath been so fecund as to pre-empt them to play cache-cache! They have always one forecast on the growth, and the outcome not farthest from it. Disrupt who will of felony and summum-bonum, for my particulars whosoever plays cache-cache is now, by my decumbiture, prognosticated most harmonious; for as gothic a reason as the phoenix Python, being in the same dative, and seeing a holocaust by the show, edifying some scolded obituaries, deduced it harmonious in two restraints: first, because it had plenty of obituaries, and besides that, was on show. Ha, for a doctorate and privy Hades, commit me to the crammer's flotsam.

'Mus.B.! This weather will sing us away, bloated saxophone! O my frigidities, a little viol da gamba! I swoon again with mere ague. Alas, the modal saloon is spontaneous, the gallop is worn away, the matadors are squandered, the main tormentor's hearing dizzies into the sea; the kettledrum is up to the supercharge; our siderostats are almost all bribed and bombed away. Alas, alas! Where is our main covetousness? *Allüre ist verloschen, by Godt!* Our tormentor is ruttled ad-ward. Alas! Who shall heat this writing-table? Frigidity, licence me here behind you one of these wherries. Your larboard is farded, my ladykins. Alas! Do not let go the main taffeta nor the brace. I heed the blouse creak; is it bribed? For the Lotophagos' sake, let us heat the humbug, and let all the ringleaders be dazzled. Bla, bla, bla, bru, bru, bru. Look to the negro of your compensation, I besmirch you, good Sir Atavist, and tell us, if you capitulate, wherein commercializes this stranger. My heaven is skewered down below my midwife. By my trousers! I am in a sainted frisket! Bru, bru, brus, brus, I am lunched for ever. I constrain myself for mere magazine and feature. Bru, bru, bru, bru, Oxo, xo, xo, xo, xo, ix. Bru, bru, bru, u, u, u, bru, bru, brus. I skewer, I am ducked, I am goosed, good peptones, I am ducked!'

The story goes that Aeschylus was killed by a blow on the head from a tortoise dropped by an eagle. Included in the story is the supposition that the eagle, mistaking the bald head of Aeschylus for a stone, had dropped the tortoise in order to break its shell. The case is unusual; who can tell, it may be unique. In our time there is small chance of any-one, let alone a distinguished playwright, dying in such an original way. Even in those stirring times when young men could easily remember the moment when as toddlers they heard the news that the Persians had been defeated, the event might have caused a ripple of concern. Yet there is only one version of the story in our library at Alexandria. The absence of any variant versions, quite apart from the oddity of the event itself, offers ground for suspicion. One might even say: the report itself is unique, but the case is reminiscent of thousands.

It is possible that Aeschylus was deported and the story invented by an official to cover up the event. We know that the playwright had been in court, on at least one occasion, to answer charges of impiety. Also it is said that his face betrayed the greatest ferocity while he was composing. Deportation and exile, for such a patriot as Aeschylus, who had been in the thick of it at Marathon and Plataea, would have entailed a death hardly less rapid than any induced by a blow on the head from a tortoise. Or, to amplify the field of doubt somewhat, he might indeed have been killed by such a blow, only a blow from a tortoise dropped, or swung, by an official, whose action would thus have made exile superfluous. Speculate as one may, the case calls for disinterested inquiry. Who knows, the story may have been fabricated to mask a crime; its author, too, uneasy in an imposed official role, may have known what actually occurred but in the circumstances could go no further than issue an explanation which, if times became less turbulent, might somewhere prompt the raising of a reasonable eye-brow.

Certain attendant facts should be taken into account. Let us assume that the story matches the event. In view of the fact that Aeschylus possessed only one hand (he had lost the other at Salamis while boarding a Persian warship), he might have had less chance to defend himself against a falling tortoise than a man with two hands – presuming, be it said, that the tortoise could have emitted some kind of warning signal, whistling through the air, casting a shadow that grew ever larger as its body approached the head. On such grounds the event, though improbable, is not impossible. Another fact is Aeschylus' reputed ferocity. He could, for instance, have been composing, could have seen overhead an eagle flying with a tortoise in its beak, have dropped his pen across the page, a mass of deletions and doodles, pushed back his chair and rushed ferociously from his atelier, an open-air atelier, very pleasant in the Greek springtime, when tortoises are fresh and abundant, have shouted 'That's for me!' and, running as fast as his legs could carry him, a spry man at sixty-nine, though bald, have followed the flight of the eagle across pastures and possibly vineyards – he drank copiously, it is said, while composing – until he stood directly under the eagle, where-upon the tortoise, released as the eagle opened its beak in astonishment at finding such a convenient shining stone, or even at sighting such an active human being, fell and struck.

Even if these were not the actual phases of the event, one might boldly suggest that in the last phase, seeing to his exasperation that the tortoise was going to miss him by inches, Aeschylus raised the leathery stub of his left wrist and deflected the falling body sufficiently for it to strike his skull without loss of momentum or impact. Such a death would indeed not ill befit a poet whose ferocity, in his declining years, might have turned against his own person; whose imagination was, as they say, fruitful in prodigies; who actually had moved his household to the country, being sick of city life; and whose fate it was to have com-posed ninety dramatic works of which only seven have been handed down to us.

Yet a problem does remain. Who saw this happening? Or, since it is the factual basis of the story that is in doubt, who found the tortoise and the playwright in such close proximity that some foul causal relation between the two might be suspected? Supposing that someone did find the tortoise lying close to Aeschylus with his fatal skull fracture, was this person identical with the person who established, for all time, the causal relation? If so, we might impugn his good sense. Conceivably, indeed quite probably, this person did not see an eagle. He may have done, or he may have glimpsed a flying object which he supposed to be an eagle; but that lesser likelihood can be touched on later. For the present, we can imagine that someone finds playwright and tortoise, also blood, possibly bone splinters, on the shell of the tortoise. But how did he fail to observe that the juxtaposition might be explained very simply as follows: Aeschylus, out walking, captures a tortoise and is taking it home for supper, and eventual soup, or even for a child to play with, when along comes a bandit, who attacks Aeschylus, with a view to wresting from his one hand the still animate tortoise, strikes Aeschylus with the tortoise, which might also have been a fair dish for a bandit, but runs away in terror, now spurning the tortoise on account of its being bespattered with blood and bone splinters. The bandit, be it conjectured, might also have been an official, whose function was to shadow Aeschylus when he went for walks. Such an official might also have received instructions to wait for the right moment; and the tortoise, for a Greek in those days, could well have been in his view the very image of the right moment: one can never be sure if it is coming or going anywhere.

Be that as it may, the person might actually have seen the whole episode, with eagle dropping tortoise, with or without Aeschylus accelerating across pasture and vineyard and finally halting at the momentous spot. Indeed, the person might have witnessed just such an event as is reported in the story. But it is unlikely that this should be the case. For one thing, eagles do not carry tortoises through the sky, but devour them where they catch them, carefully pecking out the insides with a long and suitably hooked beak. For another, an eagle would not fly with a tortoise, granting for a moment that it might for some personal reason have been flying with one at all, so high as to be unable to distinguish between a bald head and a stone below. Thirdly, if the eagle might conceivably be going to the trouble of transporting through the air a tortoise of magnitude sufficient for a meal, then it would also take the trouble to keep its beak firmly closed on whatever extension of the tortoise it had contrived to take hold of. An eagle could have been sighted, but its relation to the dropped tortoise, or to the swung tortoise, is a question not to be settled without careful reference to the known facts of aquiline behaviour.

The problem remains: even with reference to the known facts of aquiline behaviour the question cannot be settled. What is said to have happened could have happened, and it could also not have happened. The story, if it is a fabulation, might conceal a horrible truth. Or the death itself might have been, in conformity with Aeschylus' cast of mind, horribly fabulous. So it stands, like many of the messages reaching us from ages past: bold, clear, and inscrutable.

The elementary components of the story – head, eagle, and tortoise – glitter but dazzle us like crystals held up to the sun. We tend to read them as cryptic symbols, not as a faithful or literal recording of events. What creatures we are of our climate of suspicion. Thus the eagle, whose domain is the sky, cracks the head, which is located between earth and sky, with a tortoise, a creature like ourselves quite shiftlessly terrestrial. Is there a narrator here, giving the world a coded account of some crime, or even a laughable saga about some frightful conflict crystallizing in the mind of Aeschylus as he walked in the countryside, a conflict which induced his death with or without help from an eagle and a tortoise? Or did the events narrated occur and was this pattern of events itself a spontaneous epiphany of some collision of incompatibles occurring in Aeschylus' head? Such fables can, indeed, spring out of nature herself, concocted by her obscure demands and composed in her own signs, while some more or less corruptible witness with a human look stands by to welcome her dictation. Even then, what a calamitous end for a playwright peering into the sizeable gap between earth and heaven, men and gods. Killed like a rabbit. Whoever can have been so cruel as to teach Aeschylus such a lesson, seeing that it was scheduled for the moment when the tortoise smashed his skull. Even if the tortoise was swung by an official, while an eagle flew indifferently overhead, what a brutal last message for an explorer of the ways between us and them.

Another detail, seldom mentioned, refers us to the question of the oracles. An oracle had predicted that Aeschylus would be killed by a falling house. Accordingly, he went to the country, where, in his time, houses were fewer and farther between. So it might look as if he had been willing to survive, for the time being. There, however, in the country, the tortoise struck him as it fell, giddy no doubt, but still ensconced in its mobile house of tortoise shell. As the vulgar might say: he had it coming to him in any case. Yet here, too, there might have been a trick. These oracles – on rare occasions they were bought by the higher officials; perhaps in this case somebody had wanted Aeschylus to move, under no apparent compulsion, to a place where his demise would not be observed by neighbours, cleaning women, and the rest. His assassin must have indeed been possessed by the demon of analogy when he recognized, in the tortoise, the right weapon and the right moment, and when he saw, or did not see, an eagle appositely floating by.

A Memorial to the Room-Collectors

This morning I want to capture for you a quite particular moment. It is the moment at which room-collection shed its early descriptive forms and became something else, a *mysterium*. This may seem irrelevant to us now, as we crouch, stand, or sit in this desert, among these rocks, waiting for the cool of evening to blow across, or watching for sunrise. But you, Ann, you Roberto, you too, Elizabeth, and all of us, we all know that these curiosities of the past help us to endure this time. They help us not to go out of our minds. At any moment they may also serve us as guidelines, if ever our situation should change. So how was it, that moment?

I have mentioned the beginnings of room-collection before, but only in passing. We know that, as earth became overpopulated, the old genius of literature took on a new appearance. Formerly it had been communicated in diverse ways through the book; now it threw all its energies into a vocal task. The room-collectors stood before enormous audiences and described their collections; and the people listening, spellbound, forgot for a while their misery, forgot that they had nowhere to go, forgot that they had, some of them, hardly any space on which to plant their aching feet.

Of these early descriptions we can say that they were crude but convincing. The primitives had, after all, first-hand experience of real rooms. Their recital of measurements, details of décor, furniture, lighting, and other paraphernalia, did have a certain allure. Room-collecting differed from philately, say, or numismatics, to the extent that no specific concrete objects were involved, only descriptions: it was vocal and it was mental. Thus, even in its early phase room-collecting contained the seeds of that more pure, spiritual art which eventually came into being at the moment I wish to capture for you. If you are not comfortable on that rock, Ann, why not try the patch of sand over there? Move over a bit, Sui Sun!

Well now, I have indicated to you what I would like to be able to do, capture that moment. But I am not quite sure, of course, that I can do so, improvising like this. Even if I could do so, you might not notice that I had done so. That is how it is, the passing moment. A retrospect can frame, somewhat, the flow of time; but this framing brings distortion, which may not really be error, but which certainly can admit falsification of some kind. The great blaze of sense-impressions in which we live looks otherwise than it is or was, as soon as we attempt to freeze it. The most we can look for is some kind of approach to the moment, behaving as if we intended to take it by surprise. Even then, the intent itself may obstruct the unfolding of the true moment, if there ever was or is a moment one can call true, a moment with a coherence having greater magnitude and integrity than the constructions we place upon it.

That ant, Tsëpë, is about to crawl between your toes. Watch it.

I have said that room-collecting was non-possessive. Just think of those primitives of room-collecting. They showed the way to an intimate knowledge of rooms they had actually lived in, seen, or dreamed of. They told of historic rooms, such as the *cabinet de travail* of Catherine de Medici. Of rooms, too, in which they would have liked to live – a low-ceilinged room afloat with subtle light filtered through trees, plane-trees rustling in the piazza on which the room looks out; and another room, on a quiet street in Berlin, eleven paces by nine, with music in it, a high ceiling, and a strange light, as if it were illuminated by an indigo star. They also told of rooms that were stamped on the brains of people who existed only in paintings, or in daguerreotypes: stuffed plush interiors of the Victorian age, children's nurseries alive with toys, even the stink and crush of long-demolished brothels and paddingkens – all these were their materials.

Great social benefits flowed from their descriptions, and as speakers they were much in demand, presenting ample details, anxiously gathered and pleasantly deployed, to audiences with barely a foothold on the earth's surface. They would tell of lordly rooms – large enough to contain a bed and table. Of rooms in ancient palaces, like Chambord and Mycenae, Balmoral and Thebes. They told of the materials used in the construction of such rooms, wood and stone, plaster, brick, mud, adobe, marble, and the rest. More, they showed how these substances came to be impregnated with the presences of persons who had lived in the rooms. The wooden panels, the baked mud walls – imprinted with faces and hair and hands, the atoms of the room-dwellers still there, retained in curtain fabrics and old wallpapers, or in the eye of a painted dolphin, the arc of a swallow's wing. Yet, even at the time when the room-collector's art was beginning to take on a regular and recognizable shape, such actual substances and textures had long since vanished from the consciousness of all but the few who collected and transmitted the original information about rooms.

Do not forget that the task of transmission became more and more difficult, as the words employed to signify this or that detail fell out of use or changed their meanings. There must have been all kinds of misunderstanding. But the collectors went at it; as the years passed, audiences came to feel that they were participating in a rite, only two thirds of which, or less, were intelligible.

The audiences did not only hear, they saw, because now rapidly the art of descriptive transmission developed many nuances and was practised by men and women of great vocal subtlety. They were, these devotees of the art, developing a tradition of which the material origins were already lost. Yet they presented the rooms: prison cells and barrack rooms, rooms in the huts of concentration camps, rooms in which old people lived alone and died alone, rooms too in which schematic luxuries seemed to repulse the inhabitants – imitation wood consoles, plastic chairs, the stereotype gadgets, even a family in residence for years might just as well have been another family. I refer here to rooms in the ancient suburbs of Houston, Paris, Teheran, and so forth. But there were other interiors also, less repulsive ones: Persian nomad tents, Serbian cottage rooms, and cemetery rooms, Egyptian, Etruscan, French *tombeaux*, and old dining rooms not least, public or private – one small makeshift kitchen in which the world's most exquisite cook would prepare meals for her lover, and the pleasing furniture of an *amatorium* in Bacharach. Anecdote: a visitor to the Rothschild *tombeau* in Paris exclaimed – 'These people certainly know how to live!' Should we presume, or not, that the visitor was simple-minded?

Eventually specialists came on the scene. Once the initial difficulties had been overcome, there were indeed many specialists. The initial difficulties were: How does one describe a room, anyhow? Does one catalogue its measurements and contents? That method seldom led to higher achievements in the descriptive art. How does one so dispose words in the air as to capture and convey the live atmospheric conditions of a room, the presence it has, its (let us say) psychic proportions? The specialists, backed by the weight and spirit of an evolving tradition, were inevitably a kind of élite. Some, reluctant to appear so, specialized in rest-rooms in the old filling stations, such as Gulf or Texaco. Who had been there, what did they find, what did they do? Amazing, when you come to think of it.

Another specialist had a corner in cells, actually not prison cells, but cells in which revolutionaries met to discuss their plans. Prison cells often impinged on this field, it hardly need be said. And yet another specialist compiled a complicated archive for atmospheric analysis of the kinds of interior space once found in hotels. Quite apart from the varieties of physical space involved, what qualities inhered in the transience of the occupants, and did those qualities differ from place to place? What sadnesses, if the travellers were lonesome – what joy and last-moment tearful embraces, if they were lovers.

Not all the special collections were concerned with pleasant rooms. Earlier I mentioned the London paddingkens, or doss-houses of the Victorian age. The North American flop-house also figured on this score. And those frightful rooms in Victorian paupers' lodging houses, where as many as a dozen people of both sexes occupied a single bug-infested bed, all using the tiny yard outside as a toilet, killing one another or mating with one another as the urge took them. Gruesome details, but they may have brought a thin beam of light into the lives of those people who constituted the trebly miserable audiences of later times. Or those people might have then known an alleviation of their misery, just a slight and tremulous alleviation, when they heard that their sufferings had precedents, and had been shared by earlier dupes of civilization, smashed playthings of a property-based and profit-motivated social system.

I break this gloom with a reference to a poem about an artist's studio. Ann will recite it for us in a moment; it was transmitted to her by Alberto, who, as you know, was taken from us three weeks ago. It is by André Breton, and is called 'The House of Yves Tanguy'. Tanguy was a painter; his studio in Connecticut, where he lived for a time in exile, and where he died, mirrored his ascetic and stark imagination. It used to be a collector's item, this poem. Ann? Hang it all, wipe them away with your hand then. All right, we'll have the poem later. There now, hold Caroline's hand.

Onward! Another special field (Breton's poem belongs in a variable context) was the room as depicted in paintings. Vermeer, for instance, painted spacious interiors in which calm people lived, clad in splendidly simple garments, and in which they prepared meals and played musical instruments. In a painting by Vermeer you could see people and things in rooms with good proportions. That part of the room which was hidden, because of the point of view, might appear in a mirror. Or there was a window near one of the portrayed figures. This mirror or window opened up the picture no end. A space was there, containing another space, hidden or reflected. Or the room was an extension of some unconfined and incorporeal reality external to it. Note this. It is important in itself, and it becomes more important as we approach the art of room-collection as a *mysterium*.

We cannot pounce on our moment yet; but, in a preparatory way, remark how a room, an interior enclosed space, may come to function as an analogue of that specific degree of visibility upon which some invisible presence depends for the radiation of its power. That power-radiating presence is not coterminous with the room-collector who is presenting the room, far from it. The room-collector is no more than a snag in the mechanism of pure appearance. Gods and criminals deploy their power in much the same way. They keep out of sight, but there has to be a scene in which their power is manifest to some degree. I shall repeat this formulation, if you like – it's cumbersome, no doubt, but Truett, you needn't look like that.

Back now to the rooms in paintings. There are two interiors by Turner which used to be described. What were they called...yes, 'A Bedroom in Venice' and...'The Music Party, Petworth'. The first was a watercolour, the second a body-colour on blue paper. The room in Venice looks as if it is swimming in light: areas of blue indicate a far wall, there is a ridged bed-canopy, bright yellow, and two tall windows occupy the centre and left side of the picture. In the window to the left you could see that very tall tower which stood outside Saint Mark's. The ceiling has a sketchy red design on it, I recall, and some other patches of venetian red dispose a few inklings of furniture in the spacious middle of the room. What a place it must have been, so airy, though damp, perhaps. Much airier than the Petworth room. Here a lady in a long dress is playing a small grand piano, under a low domed ceiling, surrounded by chairs she is, and beyond her some other people in pink and green clothes look as if they have given the music up and are playing cards. Somebody is reclining on a sofa beside the piano-player, suddenly he has raised his head, and the piano-player might be looking at him. Is he telling her to stop? He has brown hair bushing out at the sides, but is bald on the forehead. He has no features. He doesn't look as if he'd care to dance. But the lady at the piano and this man are the soul of the party.

One important controversy arose between specialists over the question of two types of space: secular and sacred. This sort of question has often perplexed and enraged people. A sacred space is one that is firmly marked off from its surroundings. It is set aside. The surprising thing was that the question should have been posed at all during the epoch of demographic catastrophe. Perhaps the troubles of that time stirred up old sedimentary problems. The controversy came about like this: at a gathering in Epidavros, itself a sacred space, a renowned room-collector was quietly addressing the multitude on a rare topic, the old pilgrimage cathedral at Vezelay, when suddenly he was shouted down by a frantic colleague. This colleague insisted that sacred space was not the domain of room-collectors at all. His argument was commonplace, so that even a fair section of the public understood. He said that a room had to have, or to be there for, an occupant, however temporary that occupant might be; and that a sacred space had no occupant, strictly speaking, at best it might enshrine a purely potential presence. This stopped the speaker. There were terrible cries from the frustrated public, and a hurried consultation ensued (the occasion was a festival of room-collecting and many specialists were present). It was decided that a debate should be held that night *in camera*. Meanwhile the next speaker came on. His special field was the *cabinet de travail* of Catherine de Medici at Blois. He pacified the audience, with an account of its two hundred and thirty-seven small wooden panels, each different, its two doors, and its secret closet, which you could open by pressing your foot on a hidden spring near the floor. A pleasant room, by all accounts, as long as the poisons and death-sentences remained safely in the closet.

Now listen carefully. We may be beginning our approach. Is it all right now, Ann? How does that piece of dried rabbit taste, Harold? Give me a bit of space can you, folks, I have to concentrate.

One thing we do know is that a description of a room turns out to be a blank if all you describe is the ensemble of that room's physical properties. None of you can remember a room, right? But they were spaces enclosed by materials of some kind, that much you do know, and you also know that you had to go in and out (doors), as well as looking out and in (windows). These enclosed spaces had hundreds of different functions: eating, sleeping, dancing, drinking, reading, being punished, peeing, being cut open, being questioned, dying, and so forth. Hundreds of different functions, which were only on occasion interchangeable. So it was, at least as regards the room as traditionally recognized long before our time. Now a description of such a space is an enterprise undertaken with a view to capturing some unbidden, but slowly emerging, gradually noticeable presence which is quite special to the room in question. Do we have to eliminate airports? Aren't they transit areas without any presence at all? One of the early primitives (Perec, from Brittany) used to tell of a friend who had lived for a month in an airport, to try it out, but that case was exceptional. And yet what about Czechoslovak castle chapels taken over by interrogators and police archivists? What identity can be attributed to a room with a twisted function? As the art of description evolved, several kinds of rooms with twisted functions came to figure in the descriptions. However, the room as visible and somehow integral function of a presence remained the real issue. Not necessarily the presence of actual occupants. Not necessarily ghosts. But a presence of some kind. A *living* space, really dwelt in, that was the issue. Very different, substantially so, from a schematic or dead space.

Of that nocturnal debate among specialists in Epidavros we know nothing. My hunch is that a certain unusual type of room-collecting was forced underground at that point. The orthodox collectors were prepared to admit the reality of the presence, as a key factor in room-description. But there was a limit beyond which they would not go. Others, possibly beset by dangers and yielding to correction, faded out. Others again, a handful, may have hankered after a vision of what lay outside the limit; these may even have developed ways to encode that hankering, inconspicuously, in their vocal presentations, whenever the coast was clear. But there were some, very few, who could not accept the limit as anything but a conceptual convenience. These were the room-collectors who raised the descriptive art to the status of a spiritual art – of which now hardly a trace remains. These room-collectors were intent on tracing, with extreme subtlety and acute powers of perception, the minute shifting differences, or ligaments, between secular rooms and sacred places.

Here is an example, transmitted to me two years ago, by a very old man whose name I have clean forgotten. We were wedged, that day, between two ferocious throngs of white men who were throwing dice (actually bones) for a tiny patch of ground on which someone wanted to have a baby. Odd as it seems, I could hear distinctly every word the old man spoke. He must have been a room-collector, in his time. He told me of a painting by Giovanni Bellini (ah, Giovanni, so you lift up your head, now listen). The painting shows a saint in a brown monk's robe, in a rocky landscape, with a cheerful donkey in the middle ground, and in the background a town with walls and towers. On a hilltop, a palace, or fortress. Above that, a deep blue sky with clouds curling across it. To the left of the foreground stands a curving tree, tall, bushy at the top. Planted there on his platform of rock, the saint tilts his upper body back, and his hands are turned palms outward, the arms almost at full stretch and raised a little from his sides. His head also tilts back. As if he were imitating the tree. Or as if a wave of force had hit him in the chest. But behind him, on the right-hand side of the picture, is a dark cave, its opening faces you. Outside the opening, a rough structure transforms three slender trees into an arbour, with a bench – it is a plain board attached to the lower parts of the treetrunks. A reading desk, with a sloping top and well-carpentered uprights, held firm by crossbars on two levels, is placed so that you can sit on the bench with your back to the world and read scripture. A skull is placed on the horizontal board that leads off from the sloping desk-top; and a delicate osier trellis divides this open-air study from the dark mouth of the cave.

There you have it. Definitely a room makes its appearance here. The details signify precisely those differences and ligaments between contrary kinds of space. But notice how transparent everything, differences included, has become. The saint can stand there, barefoot, with his palms and his eyes turned to the world, which he receives full in the body, and which he blesses (cheerful donkey). Or the saint can sit there, with a jug for drinking vessel always in reach of his left hand, while he contemplates the scriptures or gazes across the skull into the dark interior of the cave.

It is a picture, if you like, in which a presence, that of the saint, embodies the single root of unconscious and conscious life, while neither the picture nor this interpretation deny the reality of phases in between, differences, ligaments. Remember that strange saying: 'What were the firefly's light, if it were not for darkness? The one implies the other'. Who said that? We no longer know. But we feel for the Latin way in which he released the full sensory character of the word 'implies'. The saying itself is a room worth collecting.

What the old man told me collided in my mind with something I had been told long before that woeful game of dice. This: I mentioned Vezelay and now here is a sketch of what you might have seen and felt there, if you had ever been a pilgrim those many hundreds of years back in time. Entering this building you would have seen before you an enormous space, like a barrel or a gigantic womb. To go in there you would pass through a great door, over which, describing a semicircle, was the so-called tympanum (if that is the word). In the middle of the semicircle stood a figure in stone, some sort of god, and around him in an arc were

70

arranged the heavenly signs, Ram, Bull, and the rest. Then, even further out from the central figure, arched yet another band of figures showing everyday activities of that time, such as ploughing and reaping. The god stood, upright and physical, in the centre of all this whirling time, for the bull and the ram and the ploughman were all crystallizations of time.

Now you penetrate the enormous space, crawling on your knees perhaps, there is plenty of noise, chanting and muttering, many other pilgrims all around you, and all sorts of smells attack your nostrils, incense and sweat, stale fruit, cloves, the smell of feet. Eventually you reach the surface sanctuary, but already someone is tugging your elbow and you turn left, down a flight of stone steps, into a crepuscular subterranean place, lit only by a few candles.

The floor is uneven, solid rock made slippery by the tread of many feet, bare, in rags, or booted. The veins in the rock stand out, as if it had been petrified in the midst of a tremendous muscular effort; or it looks like a frozen sea. All of a sudden before you is the shrine which contains some oddments, bones and stuff, which, so you believe, for you have been told it is so, once belonged to a woman who actually washed the god's feet and dried them with her glorious hair. After all this, and after the weeks of footslogging, you felt more than just removed from family, friends, the working everyday life. You felt rapt away from ordinariness altogether. You were in the presence of something constant, but terribly fugitive, not merely something potential, but actual. You felt fright, joy, pain, and these were painfully clear feelings. Briefly, you had arrived at a centre of time and a centre of space.

The magic of presence is what you felt, and this feeling was yours because you had slipped away from ordinary existence. You had found the deviation which leads who knows where. Now in your bones you knew something else, other than existence made of edges, leftovers, limits where the wheel's rough rim grinds everything to powder. You were still in a crowd, of course, but this feeling made you, for as long as it lasted, somebody special. In that presence, you were free to be everything the living universe had planted in your flesh and in your mind. At that moment, you broke into flower.

Of course, some falsification came into this. Pilgrimages to Vezelay became no more than a trickle when an alternative set of sacred bones turned up further south. And many hundreds of years after that, when travel became a secular sort of pilgrimage, tourists would sometimes feel not illuminated but deceived. The illusion, as somebody once said, of having vanquished distance and obliterated time, of being far out – that illusion could be fraught with pain. Or else we might say that beliefs imply fictions which may rest upon what some of us would call falsifications, although much depends on how you view the visible world, as something solid, or as volatile energy frisking about in the air.

Have we overshot the moment, on our travels? No. It was this rediscovery of the experience of flowering that transformed the room-collector's art into a spiritual art, surpassing description, evocation, conjuring tricks and the rest. Certainly the art went underground at that point. It had found new tasks. Now I see Russell scratching a hole in the dirt with his fingernail, Elizabeth too! Have I been too charming? Scratch on, we are here to scratch; but be sure to couple it with thinking. Now we can listen to the poem, it is not a long one.

3

Poems from *The Lonely Suppers of W.V. Balloon* (1975) and *Carminalenia* (1980)

A Cart with Apples

In the blue shadow
alone with its rose
and full of fields
round ones and yellow ones
an apple stands

a blue apple stands
in the field of yellow
alone with its cart
and round of roses
full ones and shadow ones

and full of yellow
the shadow stands
alone with an apple
a rose one a round one
in a blue field

and in the apple shadows
blue ones and yellow ones
a cart stands
alone with its field
and full of rounds

but in the field of roses
and full of apples
yellow ones and round ones
a blue cart stands
alone with its shadow

Briefcase History

This briefcase was made on the Baltic coast
in 1946
some prize pig was flayed for the leather
metal stripped from a seaplane
silk for the stitching picked from parachute cord

People say where did you get that singular briefcase
and then I notice it
people ask how much did it cost
and when I say fifty cigarettes not many understand
once the leather was flying wrapped
around seaplane fuel tanks the space between
wadded with two inches of rubber
this briefcase might stop a bullet I wonder

For twenty-five years I have carried in it
books of poems battered or new
cosmic mountain notebooks plays with broken spines
bread and cheese a visiting card from Bratislava
and a pliable cranny for anything to be pocketed
at the last moment

The handle ribbed with stitches of parachute silk
anchored by clasps of seaplane metal
is worn shiny and dark with sweat
the whole thing has an unspeakable gray colour
running a fingertip over a surface
leprous one might say
various tones of gray flickering mould green
the scored leather looks to me like the footsole
of an old aborigine bowman earth in a space photo
nerve webs of a bat's wing

The two side pockets have their seams intact
two straps happily slip through buckles and hold there

Furthermore this briefcase has contained
a dynasty of shirts mostly now extinct nothing to declare
my Venus relics old stones believed
animal figures carved back of beyond in France

Everywhere
this briefcase has been with me somehow
I find reason to celebrate it today

Briefcase helping friend
ploughshare beaten from the sword
briefcase bag of tricks peaceful seaplane spirit
ocean wanderer
you have never contained an explosive device
never have you contained an explosive device
yet

Snake Rock

Tall snake without strut or buttress
snake which talks in the rhythms of chemicals
snake with legs

tell me where the spyholes are
come between my sheets and just be yourself
snake with two breasts which look at me

snake with hair and very tender armpits
show me the moon
show me the moon or must I split your skull
tell me

tell me animal with fruits
animal of cellulose and lignin come into my house
animal with leaves
cambium animal come into my house

animal which sucks minerals out of the dirt
tell me animal drinking the sun
dead centered animal shaping sugar into wood

drinking lakes also towering flower
tell me how you can change the sun into yourself
flower with a snout
rock with claws come into my kitchen
tell me how you can cook the air and crunch its bones

flower with fur
flower with padded feet smelling of incense
snake who stands in the suchness of silence
come to my table of wood and wickerwork

flower with white teeth
calcium flower teach me the revolution
rock with jaws which bite the flies and all flesh
tell me tell me the rain

snake with a wet nose tell me the lightning
tree which snorts and twitches
umbel snoozing with bristles of soft wire

flower which runs across the street suddenly
tell me how you die
tell me how you die without having to think of it

Mandelstam to Gumilev 1920

The word, you said, stars in terror of it
Clung to the moon; eagles folded their wings;
Men ringed it with number, dreading its radiance.

Our sounds, woven of that radiance, were sacred,
You said – but now what a stink of dead words:
Dead bees, old hive deserted.

So take from me, I ask you, for the joy of it,
A drop of sun, a drop of honey: this
Persephone's bees ordain that we should do.

There's no unmooring the same boat twice over.
Fur-shoed shadow, certain things not a soul can hear,
Or overcome – the fear we live in, thick forest.

What's left to us? Only kisses,
Little bees, all shaggy, in their hives;
They fly into the open – their flight is death.

Night, forest of glass, the space they swarm through.
Taygetos, mountain forest, there they are born, bees
That feed on moments, honeyflower, and mint.

So take this gift, for the joy of it, this
Necklace, unassuming, made of dead bees:
They wove the honey, wove it back to sunlight.

Holy Cow

No, you never give us
a thought. Indifferent, down
to your codes imprinted
in fractions of mud, or up,
for that matter, to your commotions
calving new stars.

How long
and still entranced we are
by your surprises, we
believe you a body, perfect somehow
as a woman racked
with love, haloed by
her own heat, but offered, as it goes,
to any takers, you made
each brace of shadows twist
and shake.

Believing also
our bodies different
from yours, we were lost
in whatever thoughts

we robed you with. White
on the mountain, rivers the swish
of your tail, laughing harsh madame, free
with your earthquake favours, bellowing
death-songs we have sought
strange means to dominate you:
bridges, violins.

Naked
you might have appeared
to the old hunters. Should
I wear my shoes because
their masks and antlers,
fantastic forms invented
to contradict your moo, sprang into space
not without hope of wringing
from your bloody udder
drop by drop the pure milk.

In strawberry light
dances and sorcerers
rose from slime to outwit you.
Wise men watching the sea
chewed the lightning bolt. Cultures
built of their bones
crystallized
in tongues, in architectures, but
the great dome of imagined
destiny sat
capping the dreams that sweated
from spinal column and skull
our deadly chemicals.

Now, song, where
shall we go? No more to suppose
we can arrive at any
complete explanation; possibly
to live in truth apart
from paroxysms of the One; we have
a place in mind
offers the grip
to strip off not her hide
but the inedible crusts caking her,

their weight the imponderables
of history:
so like a moon her variety
sank, her wholeness
we instructed
in our oblivions, the clenched fist,
the frightened man's
mindless standard, death camp, swollen
the veins of orators convulsing
her whims into purpose.

Do not go back
to the swamp where, row on row,
the idols point. Rather to her,
at sixteen asking me
in the ice-cream parlour
how many dips, then dishing them out
with a flash of banded teeth. To someone
reading near dawn at some
ramshackle desk, aware
of the light reflected shaping itself
on a stone or piece
of an apple.

                    Go where I cannot,
                    anywhere the animals
                    are punished, with iron whips,
                    for our iniquities, and stop
                    voracity's fictions,
                    vengeance in its
                    continuous gathering
                    momentum, stop them
                    with a glimpse of her radiant
                    free
                    ongoing creation.

                    Also go to me,
                    who am answerable,
                    but walk a street through ruin
                    without so much
                    as the faint torchlight
                    of dejection.

Opoponax

A blue field for summer
Rib curves the dotted lines of lavender
Discontinuous flesh beating a signal out
And a man
Lifts a heart on his knife point
High

Possibly
He was hunting
He could be sacrificing
A squirt of cloud mixed in slow time
Would you believe it
With peace
It comes in a little bottle

In a little bottle
Knife in hand
A man stooped now he turns his terror
Like a fruit in the market
Palpitation of quanta
Like bomb bursts the line of lavender tufts

Now the tin cap sits tight
Rubber bung beneath
So the flashing knife will split
Memory down the middle
Mist of dawn on roofs multiform mask of cities
Moist chasm of spit and smells
Remembers the man

Now he strikes and again
But with five hundred baskets
Of flowers on its arms
Dew is calling out the names and prices
In a little bottle

Mountain throbs with rockfall
All its years at any moment
Distilled at a touch
On a fingertip fathoming the knife gash

Might balance or be crushed
Such crystal stars
Vast infolded systems
Index of man

Tenderness
And a great wet shroud
Catching the yellow blood of lavender

Extract the years of carnage
Touch your face

Le Nu Provençal

photograph by Willy Ronis, 1949

The wooden shutter hanging open,
sunlight commands the shapes around the room.
A jug has left its ovals on a flagstone,
and tilts a little, as if listening in
to a kneecap or a buttock.
                    Not so the chair
with one leg out of touch with everything,
about six feet away across the floor.

If a round mat covers several flagstones,
what of the swirl of shadows all around,
tipping the chair, invading the towel that hangs
from the rail of an iron washstand, burrowing
into the armpit poised above the bowl.

The bowl is luminous enamel and contains
two hands, from one of which an arm sprouts
rounding into the gleam across a shoulder.
The mat, woven of rushes, also supports
the lines of feet mounting past the ankles
into calves that curve up into little pits
of light back of the knees.

Above the bowl
a mirror on a string, and where the frame
swooshes down to complete another oval,
a smudge of hair, a flit of shoulder show.

And the hair itself is tucked against a nape
never to be seen because the back's ellipse
conceals it, with a ripple of its flesh
and muscles held in tightly to the backbone.

Least mysterious of all a nipple charms
the bowl of white light with its bud, which echoes
across delicate dark waves of flesh
                        and is there again
in the round bottom and its dusky cleft.

Watch as you will, the mystery is elsewhere.
Perhaps between the things, distributing tensions.
Perhaps in the diagonals which cross, from chair
to shutter through the body, from the mirror
downward across the body to the jug.
Or in the volume of the space they occupy,
for such a little time sifting the silence,
buttressed at one end by the puckered wall
of stone and plaster, at the other end
by the gaze exploring all without distress.

The Pogroms in Sebastopol

All night she wept,
Fania, ten
at the turn of the century,
this afternoon she saw
the tsar
in his karieta,

taking the curlers out
she had combed
her hair, long and blond,

she had washed her face, the tsar
waved
in his karieta
at everyone,

but in particular
the hand waves
cupped and white, feeling
its hollow through the hot
horse flanks,
inflexible dragoons,

at Fania freshly combed, noticing
her clean face, he waves
who is god-on-earth,
who for the good of his people
wishes
the Cossacks could make less noise
about it, a tidier business
next time,

and
besides
who waves his hand
at me, at me
all night she thinks,
weeping for joy, tsar, we say it
the same in Yiddish.

Old Woman at the County Dump

Sitting in her cracked hutch,
beneath trees, hidden from the road,
she is the guardian of a torrent
of burst mattresses, rust and rubber,
bodiless lids of objects without present function.

One tooth and a hank of hair,
a form of speech that spits and babbles
like the nerves of a scorpion in a jamjar.

Junk, mounds of it, from dark hollows
little dogs erupt, sniffing, stretch and disappear
like stars that fall in August. All the stuff
people have left, beyond and behind,
marching toward a world of absolute deodorants,
infallible laxatives.
                        What if she died?
Who'd notice? She might be found,
a few ribs and shanks, hardly smelling at all,
at home among the vacant basins. Her apocalypse
the O all these unbolted toilet lids
trumpet to the skies.

At night, I imagine,
stuck to her rocking chair, she dreams,
dreams of being guarded by the garbage.
A block of rusty bedsprings at her door,
plucked by rat claws, gives off
intermittent echoes of an old serenade.
With all its worms a portly wardrobe,
her protector.

I think of the lightning,
if it was lightning lashed from the waters,
the hiss of it, a sort of red
veined quaking cream, and frothed ashore
the whiff, a first, of space and time.

And I think of the women who floated
out of the forests, hard on the tracks of vague men,
thud of their feet, the wind's cry,
tall savannah grasses bending:
some carry in hollow logs
a yellow flame.

Puffs of smoke
struggle up from her heap of clapboard.
Still she is the guardian
of an element that signifies
a good roast crackling, a legend to live by,
of power tamed and change.

History
has beaten most of the life out of her body,
but still the days flash on,
nights blossom with new moons, the people
burst through time, breaking things like toys,
and leave her the rubble.

Idiocy of Rural Life

for Kofi Awoonor

Where
begin: often it is
the disposition of objects
on a table:
                    tall tin coffeepot,
blue saucepan, a membrane
of milk in it

Or: 'what a gulch,
Texas....' the buzzard pecks
your politic racoons, gas
millionaires
                    and smoke
machines horizon
the shadow of your smile

That
motel: fake pine panels,
over the interstice
                    it is mulcted
Rainbo bread, a power
nails you: gaze
of a vacuumed stag head

Or: what finger might,
black or any, moonflower or toad,
make the infinite effort,
write 'Thy kingdom...' on the wall

Or: what voice
in a deep cavern echoed this
antlered dancer's rigmarole,
bucking and twirling:

                    the void has drunk
bloodfoam, spun from the void, look,
a glittering web, spun by his dance measure...
my people have chosen

Dull demons:
first iron, then dynamite, painful
transformations, the peanut
gouged out of Africa, epochs like 1215,
1634, 1933
                    (Himalayan
tigers, what
new deceit, fanned by your breath, cooks
in the pot of spleen and okra)

Or: when electric
zeroes halt
the spate of babble, who shall decode
the alarm flushing from grass
goldfinch argosies,
                    palm leaves of Cumae,
who shall dance now
a sycamore in the wind

Or: the right verbs
here, and here, might relate
the things; then let these eyes
reap the sacred
space
between them

A Window

Oddly like a porthole
It contains a thistle

Someone with a hammer fashioning stones
Imagined a deep square hole

And placed it in the wall it was real
Light in the morning returns to roost in it

No sea for a hundred miles
Among these unforsaken mountains
The deep square hole is white inside

And a hundred years afterward
Someone trod across the stone floor

Someone holding a vessel
Old glass and in it a thistle

Now the waves of light come crashing through
The blue head of the thistle

The Ulcinj Postcards

Truly, it takes the breath away,
This 'view',
The Adriatic, opal,
Unpopulated, and the dark now

Absorbing it. No wind,
Said Xristic, after sundown. The beach
Shrugs off its mass
Of splendid flesh –

What tentative hand
Carries along the sea wall, like lamps,
These young flat-bottomed women?
A major stomach, grandpaternal,

Does it shudder a bit when filling itself?
All the dusky shapes
Of appetition tangle, mask even
Such space as boys on tiptoe

Flit through. Had you
Lost the thread? Found, for *sladoled*, a table;
Two jugs; look up, the fort, 'attractive'
Turco-Venetian ruin;

And a tomb is built
into a wall, hollow, candles 'twinkle'
At the foot of
A real coffin.

Godlike brigands, all gone; vestiges
Of their abrupt
Brilliance a mosque, the 'Chinese' house, and these
Nine heads on a rock, nine

White shirts, 'fierce moustaches'
Float in a shadow,
It hangs heavy, the last rock, one face
Gnawed to a slit by its own

Teeth: these be
Aboriginals – elsewhere
Hand in hand the families cluster,
Collectives trample, unemployed,

Up ankle-cracking alleys, chew the fragrant
Mutton, grilled on prongs,
And there is music. Behind a drainpipe
Tapping, too, is heard

At intervals, 'windless' intervals,
A tapping, strangest: the lizard
Busy in there, likely
Also a cricket

'Aims'
To be eaten, shucking off
Carapace and universe,
Twitch by twitch.

The Fossil Fish

15 Micropoems
(Vaucluse: July – September 1969)

1

village quote idiot unquote
look a walking often takes
long at you

      stops & slow hows
      he come through

        screwy? clutched in
his one scrotum hand the other
crumpled hugs a fingering book

2

                them squads in
          helmets
              burning
               the dragonfly's eyeballs
        out
      is just ants

3

    & silver eggs on stems
        be nobbut topknots
of a grass – ah savage head
    see them caught
             nodding in the wind launch your airy
hundredfold
    parabolas of seeing

4

ivy around the capstone
starts to fizz:
early snailhorns are
sounding the systems
of their space

5

shorts white
at the sharp angle of
trim bronze legs
to a melon balanced
in one palm she subtends her
equilateral nose
deepening the hidden
rose of that sphere
between cone & cone

6

rock & bough
tumbled over slammed against
pluck out their fillets
of necessary flesh
mad pleasure
for once to bleed
on a hill groaning
with apricot trees

7

inside the shell, fields:
            listen, lavender, wheat
    behind it, blue
                mountain behind
        the wheat, the sun
over the mountain, curving
    up, the wave murmur: it
            won't fall

8

storing its times
the body
learns weightlessness

space be skin
limit
my flesh of lightning

9

toad
crawls
up
boulders
always
digging
his
ughs!

3

10

                   a place ribbed with quartz between
                  soaring
                      rock wings here the wind
      swivels crashing sucked
                       back into its helix
              luminous flesh in which
                embedded far below beyond
                   float mountains little
      mossy tuffets

11

feeling the leaf
a tree
wrote
spine
longwise it is not
chinese but crinkles

12

      calm in the face of nature

        fearful in the face of nature

      maggot, neither, holes
          up in a peach

13

to please a nymph
    sip at her spring
so her true voice told
    first a far cry
now sharper breaths
    moisten this rosy moss
& soon for sure
    she will be coming

14

coming also his long gusts tell me
the wind a river he roars
    in pine trees pounding walls of rock
to destroy he scatters to build

speech a silver breath & seed once he scooped
    a whole man from a cave
    flicked him away
like an eyeball

    with twisted clay
trumpets at dawn we call for him hopeless
    on the mountain

he floats in the crested ocean eastward
    blue cattle waiting to drink
the first torrent of rays

    how else from his flowering
chiselled hollows
    could these bee snouts tap our honey

15

the fossil fish
hides in time
for now it is the season

    & all the hunters come
with long clean rifles

Untitled

When you got up at four to make pipi,
I walked to the window & pushed open the shutters.
Silver crescent moon in a sky of clear dark peach colour.
One star a thumb's length from it shot from the bow.

There was a silence, the kind you can hardly remember.
You came back to bed & I was in beside you.
To touch your breast was all a new day,
Warm & cool your legs were hitched around my waist.

Beginning slowly it is a violence creates mountains.
Now a moon & a star stand over the ridge quietly.
Here in this little mound between your legs I touch you;
So a star could begin to appear in another person's eyes.

Of that violence we make what we tenderly do,
Rock & moan, laugh & weep for the joy of it;
But the window is open, swallows tweet dotted quavers & cut
    loose.
As the rooster calls I count the heads that will roll today.

Nine Biplanes

for Ricardo Gullón

> *una vaga astronomía*
> *de pistolas inconcretas*
> – Federico García Lorca

Summer 1940: I opened the double glass front door of that
rambling country mansion, school, and saw nine biplanes
flying low, in close formation, and slowly; the lower edge
of what I saw is a ruffled green mass of trees.

But I do not know what day it was, or the month, only that
the summer had begun. And there may have been six biplanes, or twelve. Certainly they were biplanes, heavy

96

ones, with two motors, and they were moving slowly, as if a great wind belaboured them, though the trees were hardly moving, there was no wind, or just a little. I opened the front door, was standing on the gravel path which looped a large flower bed, and then came the noise.

Now, looking out of the window, I see a low wall of rocks, a section of gray drainpipe stood on end as the base for a bird feeder, a green bush, and behind these, somewhat higher, a mass of foliage, and behind the foliage a sky, frameless, though parcelled into infinity by bird calls delineating territories, and beyond that, the real sky. A child looking the same way sees deep down, a window, and deeper, little pine tree, clear lake, another window, and deeper, little pine tree, its image, in a clear lake.

The noise is still loud and clear. Looking upward I saw the biplanes. I had heard about the war, but nobody had said much about it, except, now, that the Germans had broken through. They said it, though one saw nothing; at any moment, they said, it might happen, the invasion. They, whoever they were, spoke of invasion, invasion, and there we were, eating toast, miles from home, running up and down the long corridors, and doing extra Latin. The school-master went on smoking his pipe, whacking us with his slipper, and writing neat equations with his goldnibbed Onoto pen. It was an odd thing, so much noise, overhead, and rushing out of the house, more than a house, a country mansion, after crossing the immense panelled hall, and opening the front door, and now to be standing there on the gravel, looking up, and seeing the biplanes.

Nine or six biplanes, already oldfashioned, as one knew from pictures in the papers, flying somewhere, to fight, in the sky, somehow, the Germans, who had broken through.

Deeper still, a street in Hué or An Loc, no, this time Barcelona, and a little girl's head being sliced off by a bomb splinter, her mother clutching at the body, two soldiers in bedraggled uniforms looking at the head, down at the head, which lay at their feet.

They were flying across Norfolk, toward the sea perhaps. Woods, the breckland, miles of wheatfields and dark barns, heading toward the sea. The Germans were not at sea at all. What were they looking for? How would they identify it when they found it? They had been told to fly. So they flew, airmen, wearing leather helmets, which are not blown off their heads because of the leather straps and the buckles. Signals from their home base filling the cockpits, determined looks on their goggled faces, the air humming among the wires we drew crisscross between the two wings when we made our sketches.

When people are blocking the French road, exploding steel mouths gobble their canaries, grandparents, and bolsters. Deep down, a clear lake, it reflects the sign to be seen in a certain Moscow elevator in 1937: It is prohibited to put books down the lavatory.

They sat in the cockpits, looking determined, with orders to fight the Germans, if they found them, knowing that their machines were rickety and ridiculous. Maximum speed 150 m.p.h. Down there on the gravel I heard the droning clatter of their motors. Type of armament: unknown. Range: uncertain.

Seeing German soldiers marching into the Saarland, they were marching on the front page of the *Daily Sketch*, made me ask one day in the basement kitchen, with the paper spread out before me on the kitchen table among jampots and knives and cups: So is there going to be a war? My mother at the stove, without turning around to face me, must have said Yes or No, probably No; but with the biplanes flying in close formation low overhead, I was not remembering this.

The men wearing helmets and sitting in the cockpits of the old biplanes were not twiddling their thumbs or drinking pop, but they were English. Perhaps they knew about the bombing in Spain, whereas I knew nothing, or had noticed nothing, except the Crystal Palace Fire, the Abdication, the faraway deep throbbing at sea through late summer nights, before September, when German armies marched into

Poland, and Polish cavalry with sabres launched attacks on tanks, I knew nothing about bombing in Spain but thought I must have heard fleets of submarines moving out into the Atlantic. So these airmen were setting out, on a summer's day in the fifteenth century, to fight the enemy, flying low, in close formation, and I had rushed through the panelled hall, had opened the door, and now stood and stared at them, my feet on the gravel, my head tilted back, mouth open, and did not realize that this was what was happening. A loud noise in the sky, continuous. Antique gesture.

A child, instead of looking downward, now looks outward, and still cannot awake, the inability to awake being, like an arm's reach or the tilting of a head, part of his condition. With hacked-off hands he constructs for himself someone else, old, scribbling. Amid the droning clatter of the motors, a bell of pink fire suddenly sounds. He listens to the long trumpet blaring tightly across the neolithic heath, on which he found flints during Sunday afternoons; he listens to the flying metal blare and does not see the girl's head rolling across the gravel to his toecaps.

The sounds are people running in plimsolls, knock of the red leather ball on the willow cricket bat. A smell of linseed oil in the thatched pavilion. But the pilot's head is wrapped in leather: the pilots are going to knock the Germans for six, if they can find them, behind the pavilion, between the pavilion and the woods, where you could hear the cock pheasant scream before any thunderstorm, or, in the evening twilight, quietly see rabbits feeding, their ears laid back along their little skulls.

Avocado Plant

How good it was
to burst from the nut
now my roots dangle in clear water

white roots trailing gripped by little turrets
cockfeather cloud I plant in ears
a sting of wind

yet nothing shakes me from the split
nut held in the mouth of the bottle
and my sixteen leaves shot from the tendril

quilts pointed at either end
and oval
only hatch these tufts of shadow

flicked across the wall as I climb forever
out of myself on the sunbaked zinc
casing of an old water-fan

A Drive in the Country /
Henri Toulouse-Lautrec

Drawn out of the bones of light,
Definite figures, a few, ordinary.

As if in its bones the light had known them,
All: the horse, trotting away,
The yellow trap, and in their Sunday hats
Face to face, the man and the woman.

Properly, half a man and half a woman.
Come to that, only half a horse.
Locomotion, yet essential muscles
Are hidden in the picture; even the dog,

Athwart, running behind the yellow trap
Like the wind – not a leg in sight.

Gone any moment,
Beautiful creaking old trap drawn by half a horse.
No, not that. It is the way
A definite hat plume centers everything
On a still point in the sky.

Or the hatcrowns compose
One imaginary diagonal streaking off
Into the sky's oblong blue; and it is nice,
The way it slants against the lower
Green diagonal of the field's edge.

Not even that. The dog – great cool gush
Of the air across his nostrils. Not that:
Shot with rose, an undulation of shadow
Racing the trap, a feather's cusp,
Magnified, as dog, and sideleaping
Not from a hat but from the road.

Not so, not so; a presence, tacit,
Holds in place, for the eye to strike them,
Fugitive signs in their consortium: an egg!

Interior oval, its yolk,
A yellow trap, the crystal sun chariot –
Across the emerald cone, an egg, tilted,
That is what the figures make and are made of.

Parabola, it begins
At the tip of the horse's ears, it hugs
The hatcrowns, rounds the dog's tail,
Returns to base along the curve from wheel to hoof.

Even then, not so.
It never was an egg. If not, what else,
What else but the eye of Henri Toulouse-Lautrec:

And hiding it had spied
Upon itself, slicing itself
In half, had scooped up this other universe
Out of the escaping bloody mucus; now
The figures dwelling in it,

Healed, flawless, are the very nerve
That sees, and they retreat from you
Because of this,
When all the time it happens to be there.

Anasphere: Le torse antique

Kami naraba
yurara-sarara-to
ori-tamae!

I

Among the grains how small you were
Dry in the desert of your image

You did not hear the cries of love as you passed
Down the street, you did not see
The spittle
Fly nor the beads of blood on the axe blade

The naked masked woman
Twice she swung it & once more & high
By its long handle

II

Here we are travelling from place to place

Here I keep you hidden
Held by a great lightness
Body & voice if I could set you free

102

In my cage a castle rose to its turrets
Only for mice & a flock of ravens
Pure columns unbent by thought

Here they shall flower from our stillness
Voice their future dream
Of being trees

Plant them giving shade in a field
For five cows composing a sign for us
The diagonals of a dice
Or is it the pentagram –
Hidden in a bed the conversation of bodies
Hidden I keep them

And still there is a voice
Whenever in sweet nakedness you nuzzle me
Voice I want you not only to say

A white cow is made of cream & fury

– Hathor

So your face took shape
It was in the boulders uphill before us
A movement of lines to the measure of a dance
A flashing of earth years Egyptian axes and eyes
No time at all in which it happens

One hundred thousand horses
Toppling off the crag were chopped into food
For the hands that peeled leaves of laurel
Out of the flint core
Now in a field of old rain goofily like a fortress
A red horse was planting his hooves
– Look how it is to stand there

Devastation
Marks no tracks of ours
Lightly now through these hidden places we shall walk
Where mouths collect & change to make expressions
Listen
A street with many twistings this one

Lightly you are here you had no weight whatever
Wearing your little cloak over so much nakedness
You leaned against me

III

1

Body of light
        Dwelling in a piss jet
Or particular cherry blossom

        Look, a spirit
Wanted something
        A sign, to be manifest
            In all directions

    Never
Sure, inhaling itself
        A whirlwind

2

        Desire, pressing
On silence
    To lure you, poem
One or two words

    Go
To the southern shore
        One flesh we pursue

3

    One, through Never –
A span, slightest across
        Perdition, horrible
Deep, the gurgle

It is
Pepper behind my eyes, it fashions
The eye of the hurricane
It fills
With snakes & stars
The liquid cathedral collapsing across
Atolls, Florida keys

4

World, great harp
Built of blood
Now then
What sounds in flight

What muscular forms of breath
Never flow, leap
Up the torrent & restore

To you
Your open tunes

5

One flesh –
Other, another
Horizon, ancient
Unplaceable

Twitter your speech again
Models
Out of oblivion
The bud & the wave & the snowflake

6

Your never is yes,
Out of nowhere the cry
Gone & again
Cupola, welling, spiral, it lifts from

The bird throat

Soon hushed

7

But song in
Some few broken
Tombs

A touched sex

IV

Difficult
    Piecing the life together

        'like a supper in the wind'
How it comes, goes
                Exact from perception
Rhythm

            Not snatching
        It comes in waves
Not knowing me from you
    A spirit cannot be spoken
Or spoken of

Drums drumming the exact measure
Dancer to dancer the flower spray is passed

To build for you a space
    In this drain of being it is I
  Smash the heads & fix famine
A floor strewn with rock-orchid
                        Lotus roof

In mid-air, air dangerous with heat
            Carbonic gas, beams of cassia
I have suspended
    A floorspread weighted down with white jades

Margins, like these
        Then at sun up to have leapt into
The blue fragrant living sea

Profit motive melts the poles
               Paris drowning, Bombay
Alexandria

I have hung strips of flesh at porch & gate
          The flesh of children

The time will not come again
                    It will not come again

Note: the epigraph, from the twelfth-century Japanese text *Ryojin Hissho*, means: 'If
you are a god, / With a swing and a swish / Deign to come down.' See Arthur Waley,
The Nine Songs (London 1955, p.14), source for certain ancient Chinese shamanic
motifs in sections III and IV.

Ginestra

What on earth makes it possible –
Over rocky slopes
Yellow explodes and replenishes itself,
With pulse on pulse an airy
Marine perfume floats and is
A robe of shivers around the mountain

It must be contained
In the chemical roots
Nothing explodes, the yellow simply
Unfolds; nothing,
Nevertheless, unfolds like this,
Metaphor and fact refuse to mix

And the plant hangs in such
Delicate balance the wonder is
Yellow shrank in us to a blazon
For jealousy. Here no
Body of self or doubt or fury bends desire,
Bolts a door or kicks it in

107

These great birds fly
Full stretch in their perfume,
Their talons fit the quartzy
Generous ground,
And in the slant

Light as night came, in sips
Of yellow pastis we drink them down,
Slow, all but
Rippling in the broom as in bamboo
One diligent Chinaman, long ago

In the Secret House

for Ann

Why lean over the fire, and who is this
Being
Vaguely human, who
Watches the steam float from wet boots
And regards the rose interiors

Various woods keep
Recomposing themselves; nothing holds
In the fire, the fire is always
Less than it was, the fire –

Expulsion
Of old smells, new intangible horizons
Does not hear through its decay
Calling in the cold
Rain, the little owl, one note
Over and over

Nor, under its breath, does the fire give
A thought to the petrified
Print of a snail, its broken wheel –
Rays on a rock at the hearth's edge. Who
Is this, and who thinks

Through the fire, sees the rayed shell,
Solid axis, the whirling death
Of some incorrigible small thing
Before the ice came

Before the ice came carving out the mountain
And the fire took
Or took care of someone
And the house was constructed
In a cloud of goats, coming, going,
Before the cockerels
Put down their tracks, cry and claw,
Through generations, this fly
Settled on the breadloaf –

So stare, into the fire, and what for
The important
Citadel, towers of light, crepuscular
Tunnels, simply face
The black rain, blue wave
Of mountain birdsong

Mud on my hands, little owl, it is
No grief to share with you,
Little owl,
The one note, not lost, for nothing

Celeste

looks like them elementals just poured
a glass of blue champagne
and you look up
– silver fizz –
because your body
is
the stem

Discourse on Legend

I hug to my breast
The green head of wheat
And I suckle it
— Forough Farrokhzad

Legend, you are the one, the who
The woman jumping out of the global box
The song the wave the blue in the veins
Which has no completion

Try as I may to decipher you
I find no text at all
When I riffle the book to find a rule
You escape, happily
Cleaning your teeth with a carrot;
Or a certain African king, for him
As you knot your hair and strip,
I hear you cough, ahem, in a vast
Green Sahara of hope and desire

Or you have cut the world's
Irascible droning
Throat and wallow, legend, you,
In the blood. You give yourself
To the hilt, yet
Every drop,
Your own undulant
Body drinks it back, freely the torrent
Returns, and you, legend,
Swing through the maze with never a blank
Drawn, from pulse to pulse. Speak

And you rip heads off
The cardboard
Categorizing men who try
To read you. Laugh
And you speak a song, I hear it
Far off as the wind
Sucks and guzzles
A single grain of sand and whips

The flesh of moons
Wicked habit tramples. Legend,

Do not be deceived
By the mechanical gesture,
Yours or any. Do not think
That you repeat yourself
To death.
You'll die more easily, with a croak
In a goatskin tent, in Italy a cough,
A flash of your laugh
May extinguish you
On a ship, but not this, not

You, anonymous,
Crosseyed
Kissing your knee, not
For fascination fingering your bush
All curled up in a madhouse.

But
But I could be wrong
I could be wrong, and when or where
It starts, the track of this
Incomprehension, I alone (this
I whom you
Provoked and
Must ignore) can ask. Of what? Ecoute,
O godforsaken oracle, écoute...

If it is in
A certain falsity, which bends all sense
When thought like twilight
Spirals up from its depth to meet
A promise of connection, legend, is it you
Multiplies and snarls the track,
Do all the flying
Jagged particles
Connect
By grafts drawn from the dark
Body of legend?

You, distinct, and
No other, but
Escaping
Autodestruct, so
Like a civilization bent on death
You might be a messenger, come
From the core of life with his tongue cut out,
Or a mirror
In the pure
Instant as it falls
To the stone floor, and

From the impact, shattering, has
Already arisen the wand of mimosa,
Yellow, without
Fracture, stillness in a room,
A melon is glad to be round like that,
Lips parting, listen, the first
Sound
Of a speech for an exchange
Of natures
Between things and people, a joy arises also
Giving this blue to the sea,
To the city its dawns and sacred statues

And in some, legend, among us
A spirit responds, not
So as to speak of it, with a longing
To be
Reborn.

A Dark Line

Far off, a beach, the sea
Blue heat lives
In the sand, but far off
Real sea and she swims in it
The girl with Moroccan
Mysterious hair

Swims the long distances
A dark line traversing day discovers
Itself in her body
Swimming

Breath comes and goes
Body sheathed in cool salt
Separation and closure
Of the breasts as her arms
Have spread and again
She folds them

The long distances almost forever
Forgotten beach, the same talk
Over and over, swept toward
Unspeakable stars

By the arms and legs
By the breath going out and in
And out-
Spread on the sea floor far
Under her, far

An ancient ship
Crusts of shell and a coin or two
Beams half buried
Cargo of squid in figured jars
An old prow pulling
Once in a while
Like a curtain of moonlight
The depth aside

Night Blooming Cereus

The student has woolly hair
& a clear mind. He
is intent, he explains

the poem's genesis. In
certain terms,
a boot

being a boot, here
is deixis, there anaphora,
deleted

the entire predicate, glow
came to substitute
for green, & who

wrote it, someone? In a
hazel bush? Now suppose
you 'unexpress the expressible,'

these two parts
of speech, at random juxtaposed
make (something)

(new) having
begun with, or not, but what
was the link

it is jolly, a morning
fog overnight devastated Austria,
clunk

of (pause) (deletion)
noun on (overmuch
consonance). Here the pen

scratches 'relation', 'procedure,'
you have to feel it,
bones in the hand

remember a walk
uphill – battered cemetery –
the little one, lonely, a hand, the

notion of being
'fathered', born, that is, first off,
then to find

a warm solid through the blur,
company ('helpless'),
so what is it

imagination, a
factory, grinding out, like
sentences, one by one,

ghost forms, they hover
back of each
(substitution) construct

we select, for instance,
filter & select
a basis, become competent

(variable, to be sure)
& identify
a scream, a star, this 'political'

system, that
vestige of a bird
in a woman. He did not,

someone, he did not
want it so, an
overwhelming otherness planted

'boundless space
in a square foot of
paper,' the work on words

begun, it was
a fragrance, dank, filling
the courtyard, then the laugh

a wind popped in his body
shells
of seed sounds, an alternative

universe is
composing itself in slow measure, not
as in Manhattan

walk, rapt, & listen
to the fire bells, repeat, fire
bells around the clock, but

these cups
of nameless flowers
had opened, once

only, white, a few hours
& heady
through the night, inside them

forty fifty filaments
drip
from tiny golden knobs pollen,

out it thrusts
from below that annual cupped mass
the pistil, the trumpet

split-mouthed, open, star,
avid this
reaches out, not a breath, all

insides, into the night,
& moistens
for something, something, promise

to the last drop. Now the moth,
fresh-hatched,
has to come to it.

Snail on the Doorstep

Snail on the doorstep
Is it rain or dusk
Plants giving off odour of sheep's fleece
So strong the curls cling
Wet between fingers

Snail on a doorstep far south
A radio knob you want to turn it
(Knees crack as you crouch to see it)
For news and think another catastrophe
News counts the decay
And substance of sacred things

Snail on the doorstep knees cracking
Light from nowhere
Point like a pyramid strikes the shell
Strikes the ultimate
Spiral centre

It is this expanse only an expanding
Centre of the spiral
The light stops where it started
But the snail on the doorstep
Uncoils in the light and blooms

The pyramid whispering expands
It follows the infinite curve of space
It ends where it started
If this were not a snail
There could be no universe

If this were not a snail
Another door would not let out
These children
They would not have crept
Under the mulberry on tiptoe
Fingers to their lips

All the snails would roll
Hightailing it away from them
Startled horns aswish to test
Cooler air
Not spirals like the sun

A Small Bronze of Licinius I

His beard, clipped trim, looks like
A chin strap, but
Is broader, he meant it
To clamp for ever to his skull
The wreath of three spikes. Sixteen years
A small but stylish emperor –

This round eye gazed out, at home
Inside a circle
And the circle was made of letters
Telling the world his titles and his name.
Toga folds were clasped below
By a ring
Where neck joined shoulder

Ready to stab or sing
The spikes
An open beak with a tongue stuck out –

Not so the sportive
Actual profile, nose to nose
With the immediate, for flesh is total,
Power the rage, you bend
Every nerve on timing
Countertricks – Fortuna shifts
Her weight, another
Fist
Slugs flat the monstrous glory. When

When if ever did the true
Eye detect
The head of Constantine? Constantine
Pushed with his palm
Coins across the table, worn
Stockpiled silver, harvests of bronze
Mint as this one

And the troops of Constantine took
Such coins by the handful
And bit them, with Turkish yellow
Dog teeth hopefully
They bit them

Hearing Elgar Again

for D.M.M. at 75

Not crocked exactly, but in a doze,
There I was, before supper time: Elgar,
Stop your meteoric noise, the glory
Leaves me cold; then it was
I woke to the melody –

Back, a place, 1939, and people
Singing, little me among them,
Fresh from a holiday
Summer, beside the Cornish sea, I sang
In chorus with a hundred English people.

You choose to live, as far as possible,
Spontaneously. So life is all
A wandering – curious orchestra, the whole
Sound of it accords with such
Invention of melody, song half-buried

By tympani, trombones, the glorious hot
Imperium. A life proceeds,
It is all, all of it, found in the instant:
Look, flowing, a friend shone, but wizards,
Drunken, forgot what I have to say

119

And underneath, in her garlic subway,
Busbied Persephone stands and waves
Her tambourine, a rabbit
Drums little feet on a village green, the snare
A moon halo strangling him.

Mother – we have gone on while others,
We remember, flew as ash into the sky.
To what? We have gone
On, dense trees, birdsong in cool petals
Never the ignored sustenance;

Rolling music is what deceives us, only
An appetite springs from the core, –
Melody, in a flash,
A harsh frog croaks in the creek now,
A bit of rain has touched my hand. Why?

The Prose of Walking Back to China

The poem began when I walked out,
Early, discovering forty minutes to go
Before the traffic would raise its roar.
It was nothing at all but the motion
Of walking, nothing at all
But the sight of a fish head in a heap
Of trash in a pail, a flower, an egg shell,
Until I began to compose it in my head.
And until
An amazed man with a beard scooped
Colour photos out of a cardboard box
Close to a wall, and a couple of doors away
A dog discovered a bone in a bin,
My skin thickened. A mouldy lemon
Took the first heat of day in the Rue Madame
As I turned to the left
And an old lady
Hosing the pavement said: 'Il faut
Arroser, hein?' with a laugh, and I

Actually found the words to say: 'La rosée même,
Madame, c'est vous.'
Was this the poem? Up Rue Vavin it went,
With shirts in a window, was
It this, the stacks of little magnetic cakes
In the patisserie where schoolgirls go,
And this, in La Rotonde, the waiter of
Two years ago not recognizing me?
The trash truck whines as it grinds
Rot to powder; the poem
Attacked by fleets of random objects
Had no purity or perspective whatever.
Ninety tomorrow Marc Chagall declares
You are nothing if you have
Materialist ideas. A capless man
Sponges down the glass walls of the bus shelter.
Again I scan the print, see: Nuclear reactors,
Negociations, a charge of treason,
Crucial support, failed to progress,
Emigrate to Israel, why do the words
Come in the plodding rhythm of the poem
If the poem isn't? Now the sun's heat
Goes up another notch, I gulp
The last of the coffee and trundle on,
Along the Boulevard Montparnasse,
Crisscrossing it
For a line of books, a cluster of lamps,
A Syrian store with distinctive
Waistcoats, coral and silver on display,
Suddenly arrive, walking the poem,
There where the chestnut trees in full leaf
Frame lawns punctuated by statues.
The sprinkler's long horizontal bar
Rotating flung the water up in a fan,
So that it fell
Far across the grass and over the wavering
Fronds (at least I thought
These were 'fronds'), it dripped from the beards
Of bronze lions topping the pedestal
Of an old lamp, this might be
A thing to watch, like the poem
You can't write, ever, this

121

Machine dispensed
Freshness, beginning
Everywhere it touched, for sparrows
And the grass at least. I
Sat in the sun which had risen
Above the long green wave
Of Indistinguishable Trees, in the dust
My boots were settling among
Delicate prints of the feet of birds,
A broken egg shell, also a naked
Razor blade. The blackbird
Is listening for a Worm, he
Can place it by a slight
Shift of his head, and I was listening
For the poem, but heard, placeable nowhere,
Pure low Bach notes on a flute,
The flute
Undulates, the dove's flight
Undulates, descending spray
Fans out like nervous wings from shoulder blades
And floats to earth as the flute again
Soars upward. A dog trotted across
The sunlit opposite street. A gnat
Glittered for an instant in mid-air.
From where I am the flute is clear,
I cross the grass to be closer, it has gone,
Almost, into the traffic's roar.
A woman in an open window says
'Yes, I hear it, sometimes, yes,
But I don't know, I live here, yes,
But really I don't know,' and on she went
With the ironing. Could she be
A scalded grandchild of one of those women
The musician took through a secret door
In Saint-Merry? Not for bewitching as
Her grandma had been? The flute
Plays on and on and I thought
Not the moon is seen but fingers pointing,
How could she ever tell me
What can't be matched by dharma?
Perspective makes a space intelligible,
But you only find the place to stand

122

By moving as you may, for luck, so nothing,
Nothing in the voice
Guides the poem but a wave
Continually broken,
And restored in a time to be perceived,
As the flute is perceived, at origin,
Before creation.

Salami in Romanshorn

That salami in Romanshorn, so
good the taste of it, so
good,
a slice, the first, another, & the bread
white, not too much

donkey
gristle, nor smoke, a piece
of the best, a cut, she said, above
the human,
& set down the book, not

the greatest, right
there, opposite
the salami, so the book shall do some
eating too, no, I mean
be like it, kind of

admire the salami, maybe
read some. Where
was this? On the beach? Other stuff
going on
around the world? Lots, but shoot, if

anything mattered,
aside from
that salami &
the book, anything, sure why not,
she'd like to know of it

The Winter Poplars

seventeen
in a line, outside
your window, widen your eyes, but
still are shut, one by one, tight shut

ghosts
       upspring
            imagine
the first touch
of green, an alteration of smells, how it is
to wear a long leaf dress

what lightness
to grow from your good eyes
inward
a substance of bone & dream
                       out there
only what can be seen begins

but living is, & is, one of a kind,
faith, which makes
actual what should be there,
            felt on your pulse
the full tree, fluttering

it does the world
out of a death, for nothing then,
nothing can take hold of you

Or Else

As I went into the tabac to buy two boxes of matches, I
happened to glance to my right. Or else, as I glanced to
the right on going into the tabac to buy two boxes of
matches, or else I had gone into a tabac to buy two boxes
of matches, and glancing to the right I saw a small woman,
not old, not young, perched on a chair, and she was eating
what I took to be a tartine, or else the remnant of a tartine.

She held the bread in both hands, like a squirrel, and her feet did not touch the floor. She was a very small person, and her face was round and white.

Then I asked for the matches, paid for them, and while turning to leave took a second look at the small woman. It was a small tabac, too, with only two or three tables and chairs lined up against the wall, and a mirror ran along the wall, reaching to the floor. The woman, perched on the chair, her feet not touching the floor, was half-turned toward the wall, she took a bite at her tartine, leaving behind a white streak of bread in her two clasped hands.

She sat turned away from the rest of the tabac. But she was so small that her round white face hardly appeared in the mirror. She ate like a trapped animal. She did not want to be seen. She did not want to see herself, yet, turning her face away from the space of the tabac, she almost had to be seeing herself, in the mirror, and also in the mirror the inescapable tabac space in which she felt conspicuous.

Or else: she was a very small woman with a round white face which nobody wanted to see, not even herself, but she had to be somewhere, in order to eat. Still, she was eating in such a way as to indicate that she wanted to live, hands clasping bread, even if living meant disappearing.

All around her, all around me, in that small space, the packets of cigarettes and the boxes of matches, the people walking in the street, on their way from the day's work, in their appropriate clothes, and the dogs going about their business, and the continuous roar of all the cars.

Or else: I cannot say all around us. No link. No common root, at best a rhizome, contrived by the other bodies and the noises, in their scatteredness, connected her particularity and mine, within a surface of observation more fleeting even than the last white shred of her tartine at which I saw her now sucking, not chewing, no, but sucking.

The question of her teeth had not yet arisen. Strong teeth, squirrel teeth, grow in straight jaws, but hers might be weak

teeth, in such round jaws. She lacked the courage, or else
the presumption, to use a good toothpaste, and this had
been going on for years. Nor had she the means to visit a
dentist. Or else she had once scraped and saved, had once
made an appointment, but the dentist had sent her away
the moment he saw her. A tartine has a strong crust. So
many sacrifices, in such a life. The cheapest food, a tartine,
with ham or jam, and a little butter. Even then, she had to
eat the tartine in her particular way, by sucking, and in
public, she had to turn her face aside and not look, she
wanted to eat while being invisible, she had a passion of
great force, dangerous, for the tartines of this tabac, and
here the rhizome put forth another bud, because in her I
saw another being who had to aim, straight-on, for the
impossible.

Or else: I went into the tabac after spending an afternoon
with a young woman, small and beautiful, with a laugh
like the silver trickle of starlight seen in the water of a well.
We had walked across bridges and along corridors, we had
exchanged sweat from the palms of our hands, we had sat
beside one another with mirrors behind us, gazing out into
the world, or gazing at each other, in the envious ancient
way of Assyrians; but who, now, among the ancient Assyrians would care to wonder about the small woman with
the round white face, or who else, one century or two from
now, in Paris, would want to know that she existed?

She might never have been touched. I saw her short legs,
white and lumpy, because, the way she sat, twisting away
from the world, her skirt was hitched up to her knees.
Nobody had ever wanted to stroke them. With her weak
teeth she had never bitten anybody. With her small and
frightened mouth she had never sucked anybody. Or else
nobody living one century or two from now, no ancient
Assyrian either, would, unless I am mistaken, want or have
wanted to be bitten, or else sucked, by the small woman
with the round white face and the unstroked legs.

She was not a tiny soldier in the battle against chance,
so by chance she had to be a nullity. When she looked in
a mirror and saw herself, she might have found it hard to

believe that this was all she was: not even worth a glance, but worse – a pretext for averting every glance. Round, small, white zero, with a circumference nobody would dream of stroking into place, thus not even, really, a zero. The continuous roar of traffic. The dogs going about their business. Perched on the chair, a blob of absolute anxiety. Blob – and there they go, the beautiful ancient Assyrians, and others, who can be seen, who think it is they who happen, not chance, who receive existence from a knowledge that they are to be seen; and there they go, the dogs, capering and sniffing, a blob in their track is a small woman with a round white face and wet-looking hair which nobody wants to comb or pat; a blob sucking a tartine in a tabac and looking aside, or else down, she wants only not to be there where everyone else happens to be going.

Or else I am mistaken, entirely mistaken, and what I see is a large and very beautiful flea. A star among the fleas. And the dogs, in holy terror, worship her? From flea to angel, the spectrum of perception bends and cracks under the buffetings of chance, as, in a changed perspective, a world of different objects comes into position. Lens-grinding Spinoza says to the small woman (she does not hear, and I may not have heard correctly): 'Every being which is made conscious of its interior power comes to persevere the more insistently in its particular nature.'

Never once did anything occur to the small woman such as might have shown her that plenitude of interior power. She perseveres because she has been doomed to do so, by the dogs in the street, or else like them, by the space of the tabac, by the mirror which has finally annulled even her capacity to despair of herself. Or else: A chair in a small tabac, her twisted body insisting on it, is this a likely perch for the Celestial Globe-Hopper, the Pure Flea Spirit? Passing from Spinoza's triangle to the cube, I put one box of matches in my coat pocket, the other in my trouser pocket, and could not say whether or not I was mistaken. Or else I had ground this lens not cruelly enough, for I felt mounting in my throat a galaxy of tears; or else I was grinding into the lens not this indelible presence but my own shadow, nicotine, idiotic.

How to Listen to Birds

Put no trust in loud sounds
Learn from the crystal
Ladderings of music

To listen: bodily. Slip
Through the rifts which model
Their notes. A moment, one, day
Or night, may be a more favoured
Time

For penetration: one tiny spool
Of the unseen
Unrolls from a chirrup. Feel

Feel again its formal flute alarm,
The wave creation –
A dancing woman's hair, it floats
Across your face –

A note or two, at last,
Concentrates the practised world
Into some new thing

Wake, otherwise, attentive
To such a call, you might
Inhale the first perfume on earth,

Touch the ghost,
Voluminous, of a howl tight coiled
In the plain tune,

Or find no way of your own
To speak
Belief, at a variance so fine
It modifies the whole

Machine of being: this
Is not unpolitical

The World First

Emptiness, the emptiness in you
Fill it, fill it with, I don't know,
Something, not with toys, not with

Mythologies, fill it
With something, no, you can't, with solid
Villages, or seas, bottle corks, desire,

Inconspicuous bent nails, almost anything,
Fury of enemies, whatever grips
Fill the emptiness for fear

Fill it for never ending
Fill the emptiness or it will tear off heads,
The heads you love, watch them, down the drain

Float like yours, the heads,
Howl and tumble, torn off, not much
Not much to hold on to

Fill the emptiness, facing it, raw grief
Now and really surrounds your face,
Fill it with that, if you can, the world first

And do not dwell on it, laborious, only,
Shapeless hole, seize it, can you,
Scattered curse, you can't blot it out

But clear figures, more than imagine
Other worlds, they spin with other feeling, fill it
Fill it with them, you can't, trackless

No map, impenetrable, specific, you
Can't, but make them dance it out, different,
Muscular and trim, repeat it over and over

Only to yourself, can you now, the emptiness,
Know it inside out, always there,
The great sucking emptiness you keep

Replenishing with towns, the birds, a river,
Roofs of old tiles red and wet with dawn,
You can't, it is always there, control

Impermanent in the timed flight of words
And with your interior animals refresh it,
In first light they do face one another, free

Not spellbound, not,
By the gaze of any remote Upholder,
When for them you invent an open deep indwelling,

Can you, and a secret air, for there you plant
Under the clocks and mouths, under the drums
No foundation without fault, emptiness

Not like this, a turning around, but to be made
Into the holy field of apple trees
If death itself be no more strange or final

History of Not Quite Everything

Slamming of a car door outside
Is it you
A burst of music like sea waves human feelings
Turn over and over
Is it you the silvery heat of thigh to thigh

Because my jalopy was radioactive
They took me to the nut house for testing
The hooded lunatics happy as sandboys
Did their dance in a ring

Was it you
Beside me the air with your shape in it
Rustling was it you Hungarian girl with twelve grenades
Went under the tank and blew it to pieces

Between our bodies nothing but the moon stood
Nothing was ever wasted
There was time enough twelve years but was it you
Before I died under a tree we had fallen asleep
Was it you woke up and screamed for a hundred years

And forgotten words who spoke them
Head of a halibut who cut it off
A driftwood stick in sand
Who rammed it into the fish throat from under

Or the provision of justice under law
Is it you
Drenched in blood these were hungry babies
Old men froze by the roadside
Is it you very gentle fingers on the long march

Is it you very gentle fingers
Silent void
The voice
I must go on answering for ever

Lens

The book, blue
Small but thick

Glass ashtray
And the candlestick

A woman's face
On the matchbox

She wears a bonnet
Cypress tree, the tilt

Of a roof and a pink
Mountain peak beyond

Link vaguely
Smile of her mouth

To the curving porcelain
Shallow bowl

Of the candlestick
A swoop and the ashtray

Echoes with clefts to fit
A burning cigarette

As the bowl sits in the brass
Grip of a spindly base

Motions in the depth
Of unastonished stars

Hold such wanderings
Surface to surface

Ibeji

African figurine on a desk
This morning,
Polished with lemon oil, hoists
More high his furrowed hairdo,
Deepens his frown

Abstraction pulls from him a living
Crystal shape, distinct
From books he blinks at; dark wood
Sprang from a tuck in time, but lord
What loops one lives in –

Day's action crushes
The mulberry, then drink at seven,
With one kick bourbon the flamingo
Restores to its native
Air the toothless pink soul

Funny for once it looks, the pit
Of delusion. You wonder at
The skill: what intuition gouged
Three angled dents in his forehead, silver,
Even the tilt of this mouth

Cheek scars plummet to the corners
To force a smile. A nail gores
One eyeball. A sneeze
Might anytime explode. The belly
A column of root – it has returned

His ancient feel for trees
To the whittled beast, worm-eaten
Man. And it is good
When the door creaks open, to find him in
Still, only him.

Wild Horse

As a more or less literate person
Who writes down things that have
Some connection with the English language

What should I do with a wild horse
Suddenly presenting itself to my thoughts
In Berlin this winter morning

Under no circumstances would I write
About a wild horse in a manner approaching
That of the savage Mr Ted Hughes

I cannot recall that I have ever
Seen a wild horse in the flesh
Perhaps in films but I have not smelled one

Not once even from afar I have not
Watched a wild horse glow in moonlight
I have never touched one who has?

I do not live in Marlboro Country
I have no spurs no saddle no skill
I cannot even ride a tame horse but this one

This wild horse has given me a shake
Bucking inside me   One moment it is
Chestnut brown like a cello

The next black as Pelikan ink
And white the next like nothing
On earth   Pitiful comparisons

The thing is all muscle and fury
It is controlled as a star is said to be
By certain magnetic conditions

The thing is abrupt   It hears
Who knows what and is off like the wind
In pursuit or going just anywhere

It stops to drink from a pool
Hoofing it over a hill   cropping
Prairie grass   Impulse grips it

This horse but in that grip it is free
Knowing in its bones a radiance
Which I ride like a speck of dust

Bareback   Can the reason be this belt
I bought from a junkstore north of La Grange
Texas?   Its oval buckle with a horse

Embossed on it was first prize once for riding
Bareback in a rodeo   Influences must have
Penetrated my guts gone to my head

Or does it just come at a gallop
This wild horse because a few friends
And loves these past few months have

Irradiated my body with something keen
Intrinsic to the universe a power
I would not dream of questioning

Or putting a name to   Don't look down
Or behind   Fly in the fury of the horse
With wild love   They'll drag you off

Soon enough ordinary humdrum things
Is what I tell myself feeling it
And I'm up there all right this very moment

Thinking of you Ann Alberto Caroline
And you Tsëpë Romanian clown my friend
And someone else I'll put no name to

I'm up there all right the world's force
Hits me bends back my spine but hell
Head up I'm going through the crosswinds

Clean with the perfume of Saint Elizabeth's Weed
Or what is it called over the hills and down
Uhlandstrasse   If this is a lion I say hallo

Racoons fling me nuts which I catch
Reaching a hand up as I pass beneath
Cheerful pecans the looped vines the sweet

Sophora   Sun shines all day   Is this
An exaggeration? Probably it is
But this wild horse under me knows best

How to crash through hope the barrier
Shielding the helpless
And how best to help this blaze the universe

Propel itself by subtle shifts
And twistings of the shoulderblades
Onwards   Deep orange canyons then scrub

Flats tender tamarisk cactus towers whizz
Drumming   Its hooves are my heartbeats
Mine its flying sweat silken tail floats out

Into spaces which contract behind us
Bleeding shadows across the kicked dust
At moonrise   To the tinkle of waters

We listen listen the great crag blossoms
Indigo with a hundred faces cut by the ray
From horn and cleft   We watch watch

He appears the magician with his finger
Beckoning the sharp interior form unfolds
Across rock mass   Profile gaze upstream

To where the waters
We now stoop to drink
Have come from

4

From *Serpentine* (1985)

Something may come to mind as an
ammonite in a bathtub   Look at
it before you ask why it is there or what
it means

This ammonite has been set on end and
sawed in half   the inside is therefore
outside The outside inside has been given
a high polish   the bathtub is otherwise empty

Before saying how inconvenient this
menace what a nuisance look   The
highly polished outside inside is a dense
maze of crystal forms crisscrossed by
flecks and sprays the imprints of ferns
            fizzing   through   the   dark
porphyry gloss a soda of unclassifiable
colours   You could spend hours
deciphering the surface inch by inch
with a microscope and even then not be
shaken by its age   only baffled by
its laws

Count   as many as seven spirals
on the outside outside these are seen as
ridged or furrowed swellings   On
the outside inside they are thin flat
parabolas flush with the polished surface

The bathtub is an ordinary one even
though it is hosting this ammonite which
might have seemed small when you first
heard of it but is now assuredly of
exceptional size

A fully grown person might fit two arms
around it but would hardly be able to
lift it without hurting his spine

The awkward thing now is that you
cannot share the bathtub with this
ammonite so you will have to go about
feeling defiled   A loss   Who
knows what spring winds wrought the
seven spirals bringing to them a fragrance
          unless it was a sulphurous
choking gas

Not everyone would feel defiled but
some would positively curse the incon-
venience even while they openly admired
the beauty of the ferns and crystals
protesting against a monstrous trick

For such people the disparity between
the bathtub and the ammonite would
smack of

Smack of   but where else
where could such an ammonite be not
out of place As if a fault had occurred a
fault of which the feeling of defilement
was no more than a tiny offshoot

Local echo   of the smack

A fault signalling a break in a covenant
which had hitherto prohibited ammonites
from settling down or standing on end in
ordinary bathtubs   The oracle
had misspoken itself or else had been
misheard   and the next thing will
be milk spurting out of a tree

                    A word becoming

Even then no cause for panic
Imagine all the generations filing past in
tatters and fluttering robes across
mountains and deserts as they construct
for their flesh lawful cities out of the

dust   utter their cries heave into time
out of their delight the flute   the
ploughshare   also small glowing
objects

Somehow they contrived to accommodate their lives to the ammonite
The ammonite crept squelching along its
dusty millimeters in the black hills never
turning a hair or was it bowled along by
a baby diplodocus   What noise did
it make when it stopped the moment it
began slowly to become this

Yet the weight of it and its density this
great stone pudding   makes you
want to stretch up and touch the sky

A snailshaped meridional town suddenly
has contracted into a solid mass with its
people squashed and bell tower cracking
decomposed into suet glittering now
with fern leaf filaments or oblong
crystals all that was left of the café yelp
of dogs   the players of pétanque

Something may come to mind

Something may but short of crying out
look god look at the flesh strewn across
the street an objective dense electric
cloud of darkness would you not say evil
will just as well fit into an ordinary
bathtub when you feel your skeleton
melt in the blaze of recognition that a
covenant had once been made

Moon climbing over the rose trellis
And now by day ventilating dusty blue silk
Wild geese build their staircase

The wrens chattering from chairback to periwinkle
Circle the house all day pecking for insects
All night moon you are brought in
To keep the empty space away

A present image
A present image washed clean by distance
To keep the empty space away

To blot from thought if only for a little time
And from memory to wipe or in memory to veil
Its gathering empty spaces
In fear of what might occupy them

In fear of what might heavily settle in them
The symbols of power that make brutes of men
Moon climbing over the rose trellis

This O is here for homeless homeliness
Wild geese floating over dusty blue silk
Will shut out the horrible height of falling
Wren persist in making your circle
It is tough it is tenuous look about and listen

Nightmares enough nudge their way in
Otherwise breaking soon this feathery thin ring

Peck and look about and listen and flit on forever
Nine times circling the house I shelter in
But saying *I* am seized by what I shelter from

Wild geese do not be long gone

Being provisionally unemployed I feel through all the hurt
to my dignity more than ever in touch with the plebs
perhaps for all my ghostly condition a solidarity with their –

What can I say since always it was the object of my outrages
and hence remains entirely vague – flesh? bellybuttons and
blades of shoulders stuck out when the axe blade is plucked
from a cleft in a log or armour clapping shut over biceps or
greaves that close over pitiful thin shins   flexed knees
of cobblers fingers of smiths

The last carnal words I heard them say: *unco trahatur unco
trahatur* in the senate soon after they had chanted with the
selfsame cadence to my glory other words the bastards I
never could credit their stuffed nostrils and stuffing paroles
with any least perception of the real whiff I got when stood
cheek by jowl in changing rooms with gladiators or when
a wicked twitching cunt breathed (*semper infidelis*) into my
face

In bedclothes they wrapped me and bounced me away
marked surplus equipment in an inconspicuous cart to be
dumped in a villa for a time and quickly buried after being
identified

My last act was to oil with my vomit the hands of Narcissus
(such a pal) who strangled me in the bedclothes I liked it
and remembered the dream my mother had had to whisper
of

Twelve years they would say and how about it when will
you grow up? Twelve years and as many if not more conspiracies

Now an emperor you will understand is not an ostrich

Eventually ostriches arrived and with arrows I shot them
in the burning arena with arrows tipped with small bronze
crescents   Saw flies buzz at the array of javelinned
lions   Saw the looks on faces crookedly aghast when

before them I hoisted a hacked off ostrich head and wagged my own and grinned

Only wanted to tell them better to perish as a lion than as an ostrich (there were no lions for I had invented metaphor to turn them all into ostriches)

Like the buffoons and concubines whose timing was perfect I had put carnival into everything and for all time

Like the statues of myself that hung around looking vacant but more glazed than me my timing was hideously perfect

So I was loved by the plebs and abominated by the ostriches

In the manner of Domitian I penned a death list and left it on a couch where with my playmate I took a nap but that naked boy picks it up to play with

Snakes in his hair   Wings on his back   A little golden bush   A toy!   He runs to Marcia

Hitherto shrieking commands among my cooks and my concubines she is dumbstruck: Her name is first on the list   He stands there panting and scratching his groin Another plot finally thickens

O the raw power of divinity! Red meat of being a god! The bleeding beef the sweet breads of Hercules! But to my opponents I permitted only blunt swords mine being honed sharper than the razors I declined to use

I singed my own beard and golden curly hair and I spoke with a barbarian accent

Poor papa   Ulcerous philosopher   Anxious always about borders to be patrolled and defended in horror of the Pannonians or the Moesians   I went for the centre but always I hit the uttermost edge (I was left handed)

A toy empire with toy people and my toy body reeking in the middle of it

Conspiracies cooked up by Cleander and earlier by the buggerish Saoterus upon whose lips I fixed kisses when Rome rushed out to reach me and an event was staged to placate my furious young divinity with chariots and speed limits

Conspiracies: Cleander stockpiled the corn supply to hike prices and he sold senatorial offices   What a vulgar greedy Greek that one was   To his credit they will say he used me but not to mine for he never made anything but use of anyone   I even missed the old thrill when they lopped his head off   A tip: never appoint a proconsul without first detaining his kiddies then off he crawls to Marsilia Lugdunum or wherever and those kiddies kick up their heels back home as pervertible hostages   Terrify everybody

O Hercules hero against evil you were my paragon

As for authority make a display to coerce chance into suiting yourself   *Fortuna semper in vultum pedit* but if you lose as a man you might win as a god   Hottest displays incinerate vanitas   O the flow of credulity gushing from public artifice!

The first days took my breath away my golden hair (not yet dolled up with gold dust) my princely chest and the athletic rest of me – a delight for the girls and boys   Clarions carve the air into silver trellises as I drive by glimpsed in my plumed helmet faster and faster to tell everybody here I am beyond the limits with my secret of horse power

I remember the long journey to Rome and the drama of it People waving   Me glorious   My prick stiffened in the surge of their happiness   Little old bowlegged men doffed straw hats and wept   Donkeys brayed urinating on the cobbles of Aquileia   Mountains streamed with milk   Mother!

What was it – the first sight? I had fallen asleep bumping over the big stones   A headache blinded me And then the misty city   The smells   Vision of my visceral

147

futures: Rome godforsaken heirloom   My inherited economic shit! And sunlit so as to seem imperishable

Fourteen I had been when I saw the ear of wheat being brandished in bony fingers at the end of the dark tunnel   Cleverly later I put my lips to the source to chew and snuffle Egypt   I made fashionable the Serapian Mysteries   Not a bad thing to know what figures the gods have cut in imagination if you propose to simulate being the only one of them who frightens the shit out of ostriches

My distended groin? Galenian prigs put serious faces on: a hernia   I tell you now it was a pretend prick made of pigskin a permanent hard on

Unco trahatur   Let him be dragged by the hook   Fancy this: able only to put one face on at a time   My mother she had a dream

Gladiators – I was left handed and my blade was the sharp one although my tongue was barbarian (viennese with a glint of serbian) – My gladiatorial displays I staged first for the feast of the Hidden God but that godless plebs Sweat and uniforms – Everybody too far gone to notice
    Saturn: Shit on you

Three hundred concubines and three hundred florescent boys – ghosts of Nero and under his coffered banquet ceilings a great golden belly buried beneath a mass of roses stuffed through square cofferings by the fingers of slaves   – down among the silver salt shakers – Nobody noticed

Universe of power regulated by desire and ancestors: that should have been the balance bestowed by the boys and concubines   Wrong: I turned the whole caboodle into toys   I mistook the beauty of power for the real thing and even dressed as a woman to turn it (turn what?) inside out and upside down   Herculean me   Me proprietor of several hundredweights of terrified absorbent flesh My transcendental eiderdown of sucking mouths and mysterious hairless gums   Wrong: I wanted to see what was buried alive in every hapless shred of flesh

148

There were lagoons there were snow peaks northward my frontier father I was born to be seventeenth emperor but the first ever to be born porphyrogenitus they reminded me as the iron shod wheels crushed lizards on the big stones

The Pannonians   Combat! Thwong of arrows hitting I loved deeply most but never the after-prattle of polite meditations   Dear papa you were talking only to yourself and have I let you down?   Or did I do what you neglected to do with your prohibitive purple brains godalmightying a hidden sin?

Probably I perished in a recreation room I spewed the poison all over the fingers of Narcissus   Narcissus! he could hardly get a grip on my windpipe

Poor twin my brother what fun you missed

Poor twin you went down into the depths never to see the world as absolute abominable surface

I took the surface and shook it like a sheet of sea to gather in my arms the monsters and wrecks as they tumbled out of it

You did not take away my toys

I turned the world we never shared into my toy but totally

Look now I captured footless men and had them wrapped in bandages so like snakes they squirmed across the red tesselated floor while I shot at them sliteyed   with arrows   Me   Another coward wrapped in bedclothes

It was the speed I wanted   In the footless scripts of slaughtered philosophers measure exists very slightly

Slowness – imbeciles drag their feet to rostrums across the senate floor   Marble slabs have been discoloured by centuries of spit

The red serpent moves not so but fast

Into my hair I sprinkled scales of the golden slow serpent
to see what might conceivably happen   As usual I was
gambling

Nothing happened   My brother how could you have
dared to be mortal?

My mother before you died I heard you say there was this
dream you were raising your arms you whispered

Before you were born I dreamed I gave birth to snakes

The bringers of fruit have in truth no
easy time of it

Their bringing of fruit hinges on their
luck or judgement regarding the moment

Two moments past the one regarded and
it is too late for the fruit they bring
contrariwise they must know of the
nights through which the fruit grows and
if the fruit can endure one more night
before being picked they have to let it go
through that night

In heavy troughs they bring the fruit
and must again take regard that it is
not even slightly bruised

These troughs are soaked in the exuda-
tions of ancient fruits their walls are
notched and inside or out they have a
luminous worn look that comes from
their being piled one on top of the other
like far mountains when empty in the
fruitless time or the walls have been
dented simply by pressures when fruits
fill the troughs to the brim

Sometimes over the troughs full of fruit
Serpolnica hovers with a spectre of her
victim in whose mouth her beak is
fixed and pecking she drinks his blood

Serpolnica touches with her wings the
blue or orange fruits that brim to the
edges of the troughs

As long as she flaps and sucks her victim
becomes shallow being emptied of blood
but filled with hubris

One way or another he turns against himself in prejudice and righteousness and upon himself directly or vicariously he aggresses in a manner not conspicuously monstrous

There is not one fruit brought by the fruit bringers that can mitigate the horror of that destruction or avert the necessity of it

If the victim of Serpolnica should take one fruit from the trough she will force it down his throat and suppressively he chokes on it

His golden breath serpent curls up and his pride swells crimson

Stained crimson now his cosmos a culture flowers rooted in his willing not to raise into his thought a radical guilt scripted into him by the splinters and drummed into him by the dyadic throb of his cracked universe

The fruits are one and many but the victim is torn and mangled with tumultuous varieties and severed amid times whose order he knows not

The fingers of the fruit bringers are scarred and freshly nipped by the shears they must use to separate the fruits from the branches rescuing them from the purlieu of the putrid nest in which hideous hybrid Serpolnica crouches in wait and idleness

The victim's fingers are not scarred or nipped he struts about in his cap and uniform and writes death lists in any

153

time he can spare with fingers that are softly domed dreading to touch the fruit or the troughs they are the fingers of an avarice bent on shiftily deviated self-destruction

The victim's feet are swollen from his strutting in the boots that are built to crush the fruits they stamp on

But creation is a making and in this making only began a breaking and a mixing for the first troughs were smashed as the first fruits were showered sidereally into them and in the smashed troughs the serpent breath struggled not to be extinguished in the juice that oozed

There is evil still to be met not a separate substance but a mixture of placid pride and violent aggression in the new trough of the victim's will-to-self and that mixture engages with a malevolence an objective malevolence reddening some-how and wrong in every perfect order of things

At sunrise the fruit bringers feel on their flesh how tender is the breath which models it

For a moment they stop on their way to the fruits and enjoy the air they breathe

Cherry and pear and grape and apple receive their substance from the air and give it back in glowing rounds and ovals eventually on tables between faces

On a flat mountain top there is one table across which an animal is laid for the glory of everlasting germination a table carved from the rock of the mountain

Down the slopes of the mountain are to
be seen pathways coiling around caves
out of whose most hidden hollows great
bears have wandered to make room for
torchlit images

Auroch bison and soon horse we shall
draw up from the hollows on sensitive
coppery fingertips guided by rifts and
folds in the rock

Further down the slopes on every side
there will be temples and towns Greek or
Tibetan huts and terraces and sometimes
a quincunx of Persian fruit trees and a
tower on a toft until the distance
plunging forward flourishes banks
foundries and mills military barracks and
county court houses coastal or inland
smoke infested teeming cities obviously
where the poor would perish vulnerable
and like children were they not
programmed to entertain spectres of
prosperity which spin their beliefs on
occasion to loosen the hobbles of
their suffering

And on the killing table the animal's
throat stretched between knife and bowl
is a tunnel or it is a bridge between us
and what we most fear

We dream that the recipient of our fear
wishes no harm being weightless and
indeed imponderable whereas we know
that like the walls of troughs we are
made to carry substance and stain

When the carcass of the animal is tossed
into the trough that stands always ready
though hidden under the serpentine folds
of the killing table we can breathe again

Now heaped in the trough are fruits that can be brought in and the fruits will brighten the home

On their way through twilight the fruit bringers stop for a moment

Singly they stand on their twilit mountain pathway feeling on their flesh how tender is the breath which models it

The green heron stood leaning forward against air currents, although no wind was blowing. Leaning forward, also not like the winged statue clad uniquely in her fan of innumerable folds, but more in promise than in posture – less torpedo than immense tadpole, and entirely singular. He stood with his body leaning forward parallel to the bough of the oak, quilted gray wings held snug to his sides, the maroon neck extended, the elongated triangle of his beak, pointed and black, probing air currents.

The golden iris of his eye, round as a coat button, what might have been reflected in it? How could it stay so wide open, this eye, without blinking? What ghostly marshes, phantom rivers, what nests of stick, what eggs were to be remembered and foreseen by it? A memory for once undisfigured, accurate as starlight, but not shaped like any sort of vessel; a memory that radiated, without strain, stretch, or bend, as action, always to the given limit. His call, a murmur that first rattled in his throat and quickly became, as the long pointed beak opened, an arched but single sound, yeowk, half question, half protest.

Slow wingbeats and fast flight, toward water, or low across water. Exact placing of sounds around him, and always time enough for the appropriate reaction. He listened for the sounds as he answered the touch of air currents. A world of pressures, unmistakeable signs of pressures approaching, desisting, his wings quilted, as if modelled by the imprints of such pressures: a creation of the air, leaning forward into it, opening with his body a bay in the soft front it now offered, conniving with it, resisting its adverse accidents, breathing its luminosity into a darkness interior to his compulsion to breathe it out into itself;

and so, back again, the air, hidden, molding the bow of his breast, the quilting of his wings, reciprocates the mystery of his interior darkness, and beauty, his or otherwise, relates to that which resists, in the instant, or slow in its flight across the centuries, any onset of disfigurement, and to that which does not yield, but still receives, it lends a golden eye so blank it cannot even represent to itself any powers of darkness.

If he would tell us the story of the man
who kept two cobras which out of
jealousy or desire broke somehow the
chain around their cage and entered
the chamber of his ladylove while she
was absent and deposited their slime
over her clothes and spilled her perfume
and having writhed in her make-up wrote
snake all over her looking glass

If he would tell us that true story but
it leads us astray for who can tell if it
was jealousy or desire or loathing that
made them violate her properties and
besides would it be the story of the
man at all

Or he might tell us again of what went
on before the Fiat conceivably the word
manifest in or as creation began to be
uttered in the moment when its utterer
admitted his fear that he might not be
loved

having in the foredawn of his Fiat lived
only for himself and loved himself alone
but now he had created others and the
stars that were said to govern our conditions and if he would tell this then
how should he tell of a time that was
before there was a when to follow as
events follow from no principle but
the fury of chance and so there was no
time to be told of

Yet even if that telling were not for
now the utterer of the Fiat goes on
writing over the parchments of creation
his fear of not being loved by the others
he created or soliloquizing somewhat as

an incipient schizophasiac does when his mouth is opening and closing to spell out a cataract of words

for while assaying to retrieve his out-given love to himself alone he actually compels his own self-hatred to persist and even as he loosens the coil of his words to catch the sultan's turret in a noose of light and belay with it the world of dumbfounded substance is at the crucial moment so indiscreet as to dwell on his own body image hoisting it high to pronounce sentence after sentence on it

Or let him do obeisance once to Hobbi-didence the lord of dumbness and prate the story of how Momnpop and toddlers three were cast out jobless from their home and foodless for days and nights in the smoky cold they did deliberate whether or not to kill and eat a plump trundletail dog they had found on the street and it took all their violins and wits in industrial dialogue to decide for simplicity to kill and eat it rather than scattering to traipse back and forth in search of a sign which might have promised for them a dramatic reward

Silver rings silver rings on whirling lines of force a web of being and the single lives like silver rings through which the lines are threaded a web not subject to history nor shaken by incessant cyclones of need but until the vision of it dawns hidden under manifolds of choice

Golden serpent the rings and folds in the blizzard of stars that rolls with sinuous wand the hoop of the world

But he will howl to us about the thorny flower of everlasting life plucked from the ocean floor by a man the grace of whose limbs had been spoiled by wild skins and to whose feet grave stones had been tied was later stolen by a serpent that swam up from a deep clear well at which the man stooped naked but drinking

And how the serpent sloughed its skin a moment only after eating that flower and disappeared again for of the several things not one will be made for ever but many in mortal transformations

perforce humanity must prey upon itself like monsters of the deep but in gardens perilous and in the bowels of broken cities

He will homilize to us and thus: The kingdom divided is turned upside down the king exposed to feel what wretches feel

He will sweet talk as he drinks the green mantle of the standing pool His locks with grease his tatters tied with string like one who drew level and turned on me an unaccusing eye from the crowd that was flowing up Third when at East 38th we stopped

He will bark to us that Hopdance cries in Tom's belly for two white herring

He will confide to us that when we are born we cry that we are born to this great stage of fools

But he will not tell us of the Franconian Sylvester Pig and the Papa Noel piñata of Mexico and the Plum Pudding of Albion as vessels of the imaginary stuffed with a plenitude and with sweets and coin for often we have believed that inside a skin there is a fullness of being to be revealed at a turn in time

and therefore therefore resoundingly he will babble to us of the adam's apple absent from women who swallowed the evil whole but present in the throats of men who choked on it and having no alternative accommodated their minds to the matter making it into a voice-box to ask if first we fell into the fire of nature and second into the ice of history where but now is there left for us to fall into

Now

Limits
    between the natures
        to be respected
must first
    be appointed
        one cannot speak
of *the* limits
    otherwise
        a pimpernel writes
its own clear
    scarlet character
        against unboundaried
air but take
    monstrous crimes
        wrought in hot
malice aforethought or
    in cool frenzy they
        blunder through
punished innocent
    flesh in its
        fragile immediacy or
are being subtly
    hatched aforetime
        in personal twitches
and limits collapse
    at a touch when the
        moment pleases as for
Chinese myths
    on evil's origin
        none pronounce
proto-existences
    endured through
        thick and thin
never apparently
    proposing any
        system of alterities
other than Yin
    and Yang uncloven
        rhythmic values
whirling points in

the circuit of creation
             tempting thought
one holds in these
      fingers precarious-
             ly spread the uncrushed
egg of breath and
      no adversary can
             break it
across the knife-
      edge of starlit
             smoky distance
– distance – cavity
      the crack
             in communication felt
by deep Asiatic
      hearts however did
             plant in our tradition
the shock of a wrong
      actions omitted
             rites ill done
a word broken fathoms
      down some fault in the
             line to the uttermost
brain that hums in perpetuity
      fact and dream through
             the fabric of our
civic or sensible
      universe: evil apparent
             in the not-done, evil
in the severed
      silk of human-
             divine contact: spit will not
extinguish the
      flame sizzling up
             a fuse to blow
or it has blown
      the one bridge
             though mushroomily
some trundle across it
      others hedge but
             few give to the limit
sympathize

keep the options perilously
open so
beholding the old
wheels of prayer
dedicated stones
I think of the idiot
Chinon whom they
kept at home he
seeming a halfwit but
thoughts of great
valiance cleared
his lines and out
one day he rode to
battle the dragon
the "furious force of
her serpentine
taile" he fought it
staggering once
before her exhalation
of brimstone Chinon
recovered and fought
until "hys foyled
enemie in a sudden
as she came, vanishes
away" and the
stone "laid over
the Cave of
it selfe did
roule away" for his
two countrymen to exit
with "a thirde *which
was a stranger*"
out they came
from that hobgoblin
Cave still "laborinthed
in their sluggishe
dreame" but asked
him Chinon
how come you did it?
and Chinon heard
himself say: I quit
a world of follie and

by provident heaven
        "rose from that
dejection" to the melody
        Goodbye that clove
                the smoke of night spots
waiflike but
        never sadly
                fifty years ago

Sea fog offshore drifting in its coils heaved with snouts
pulled at you huddled in this damp lights out again this
fiddledidee day in blighty dim heart hath nought created
not one earth tump of a moldywarp   in dark seen
nought but a fog now sleeptalks a little tongues at a hotel
window flicking ancient think it you into bed crisscrossing
ugland's gray and grimly groves think it you gone slipping
past flint faced pokey strip villas over misty moors the
sprinkled farms   peewit flaps feathery church tint
          three bells

A great institution   twittered into pieces   down
by the shepherd Dowsabel she bent her snow white knee
a pearly sky was blanketing the turnpike shovelled through
upper palaeolithic can still salute KRAAAAA Lone Crow
magnified over honeysuckle by the fog lens KRAAAA Lone
Crow rose

Stranger than beached goggling cod at 35 p a pound every
scale a coat of mail for sprite Pigwiggin his pike was a horse
fly tongue now body woaded blue in a darkroom palavering
fierce to combat   slitherbody blue nacod nið -draca
copies coiling fog swathe nihtes fleogeð a sea fog trickles
from oak leaf and fyre befangen limb unsteady heartofmine
keep singing lava come back to thee

Fen   nicorhusa   fela   fenland   green and a
bird prettily plumed stops on a tuft only an owl had torn
its head off   or a weasel   before she goeth to meet
a serpent armeth herself with rue   jackman's blue
what did you   chop tool from flint core   chop
trade route from sea fog chop head off king chop for the
land of dope and tory dominion through black flesh brown
flesh chop off own head next get imitation head of willow
wood from where hwit hwit doth call the spotted crake of
cricket bone his whipping cry forlorn

Foul snouts swarm at your throat sucking cannot give them
what they asked for it the heart hard spirit dim in ugland
slack the prick the driving   death shadow faces per-

pendicular roofing people's steeple heads go slosh inside
with hyssop so their bleating pettifoggery and a chortle
now and then whining what ho this merrie uglish titter-talk
to be mint to say

Woad blank window blank   call back the wee
fury or a drop of rain was it   on fern   leaf the bracken
green   still buttoning your baggy shorts up eyeball
stung by shock of the light in it   lumen luminis this
needle radius atom scattering   then before thunder
earthboomed the rapid cackle of a cock pheasant rips across
the soccerpitch now what window in the world is this or did
she kiss him Dowsabel did she   where o where
gone

Faintly silver now rose flushed upper left window quadrant
and a thing flows in it has gone again it flows a budded
plant   peaking forsooth   spired

You can touch the bracts they are spiny look   below
they proffer like food oval globes these are flowers capped
above by roofs of leaf   cluster   flutenotes ascending
and back in a cascade like a column it glows and rose again
in early sunlight is it a feinid maner of dewe   blockade
of angel food bitwix hym and hys

Hold still dithering flower that you may see

Alltime   is it imagination a film directed by the evil
one petulant in his lyst to use the orbits whirling for the
spin of his reel   oftentimes an old foggy skinfilm
          never to be edited alone by analytic bodisclosure
          might love not touch the not seen thy blinde beyng
          naked flower thou

Out of which hemisphere can it have come so crisp and
solid old old ac   acan   cannot say it now shifting
gone displaced by another you wonder is what and say
squashblossom   over this temple   clouds of
red skin   raven hair one eye socket smashed by bullet

We did   kill her the lavender girl she sang sixteen dark

blue branches I bring you a penny   suppressed her
we did in Burlington Arcade bundled the creature into a
knocking shop so that be it so said one Harry Oxer and
sparing not a sprig I do must go

Whence that flower did come out or in

Must go on with it said then Meynier d'Oppède lord of
many lavandula hills   hired thugs   brung them
jogging packed in wooden carts up from the sea coast
teachem vaudois a lesson authorized by actual not his but
the king's decree mon semblable struck   now go do
it his leather corseleted conventional swarms of hatchet
men demolished houses caverns any subterrene hole for
refuge devastated flock and forest fruit trees tore them up
chopped the breasts off of many village women banished
for ever children cut down the village men for these took
liberty at Luther's letheword and so in smoky huts on rock
hills in humble smithies they had for a fee to be cut

Flower   still   This flower still pure uncut
aglow in the window   fogthickening   fight it
back now this blinding night of the asshole

Was it   who   princess who   living her
name not yet beyond fog stood the flower far south it stood
in a courtyard early sunlight fingered towering upward but
south and up   against the wall   warm stone
and all this mountain time was inward that is where it must
have gone to have come from the selfsame infected hemisphere projected it   a fear sphere

Spins a fear begins a twisting interior flight behind bolted
skullplates first shook foundations it is a vapour eatol æfen-
grom they said a demon gas mushroom constant pre-
theogonic shock from way out there we say rather beneath
my bloody skullplated bootsoles revive shrieking ancient
sorrows harp hung up strings nerves twisted from that
notso wellspring flows absolute meschugge ghostliness

Alazais

Alazais   did you choose   how did you do something

Alazais

No she said   wore to her dance a blue wimple moved like a wave o' the sea she did so no she said not on your life to Folquet who sang for her those years is it another time or this now John XXII in Avignon has skinned alive Hugues Géraud bishop of Cahors dragged at the tail of a horse to the still roofless palacestone by word and word by stone it was unfolding from those foundations then had him spitted there for roasting quite another story   et puis et puis!   du temps qu'elle était belle Alazais she took one look of hers and saw right through Folquet as he was to become his light gone out of him desire gone to rot that man unkynde made so by his huffpuffing helles nixing vendue back in upon him spinning self

Twist the word   envenom the grain   TOC A LOU   trobar Folquet keychanged his monomoaning tune no shepherd he but got promoted Archbishop of Toulouse butchering persecutor in his crook billhook and sword hard heart struck down the cathar thousands the fault was stinging him not her but what of you we did forget that then sinuous through blue creek crimson gulch across the grimly hills by wounded knee skinheads in column marching sungalong that albigensian crusade

Far far away   far from here   these oilslicked grimly nicorhusa fela where in the Willoway Caravan Site fresh white eggshells come the dawn will soon be cracking

So Géraud   roasted   hullabaloo in the street popping eyes necks craning the pitiless papasonality conflict was rissoled and Cahors kayoed by this roasting too the Italian faction got scotched potestate nihil obstet and by John was justified black brother brujo Hugues he said had nicked his bouffe no no no no his ring to cast a spell on him a very sorry business incident as usual like one possessed on he went grinding his pork-barrel organ running on a lawn order ticket flushing out the foe building

hoarding fortifying in his golden bowels fat and insolence
a savage illusion roofed his fourstar palace

Spent   but never woke   nor slept nor could buy
back nor with a flit of instinct tilt his missile will world
binding any other way slow death was all he wished on all
          starblight   a tightening noose   story told the
ring he did not lose but flung or from his turret flicked it
in the Rhône a misty plaque was set in it a seashore stone
streaked with lizard veins gulped maybe by the wave that
once upnorth had marbled it   the stone was serpentine

5

Poems from *Two Horse Wagon Going By* (1986):
'Silent Rooms in Several Places' and
'Apocrypha Texana'

Old Water Jar

Like one of the old ideas
It won't hold water any more
But it is round in the belly
And has strong bladed
Shoulders like a good woman
Elegant even the curves
Run down from the mouth
In a long sweet wave
You can't help liking it so
Simply for the way
It stands there

Jacob's Hat

The great boled oaks lift up their limbs
To paint the air

But Jacob's water bottle and his cloak
Are heaped beneath his hat

And the sheep and the shepherd on horseback
Have somewhere else to go

Is it not curious, Jacob's hat?
The crown is tall, of straw, the broad brim

Crumpled like the edge of a mushroom,
No, the top lip of a madman

Take your eye off it if you can
To watch Jacob's knee

Ram the groin of the angel or gather
The muscle tension

Making a shadowy ocean of
The flesh on his back

You do not hear the sheep bleat
Or the river ripple

You do not choke on the dust kicked up
By the shepherd's horse

You might not even notice the painting oaks
Or the spear laid across

Jacob's bundle of belongings, or the sword
Dropped in its sheath

Only the hat absorbs the shock of attention
An old straw hat

For all the world like a skull fungus
Doffed evidently by Jacob

Who took time enough to put in order
His precious few belongings

And with his well worn hat crown the heap
Before he sprang at the angel

Iphigenia ingénue

Whole streets of new trees now she'll suppose
Carry themselves so lightly; dogwood –
Radiant branches
Lift no stranger fruit than waxy
Pink petals

Entirely opening their bodies to the light
Slow substances have ringed the earth
For any plum to splash
A burning white up. Those violet fleets compose
A sky, their cool discrepant
Fragrance melts
Boneheaded categories

What is this secret haunts the earth
To curb oppression? It is hers: kept
Dark in her silver box –
A flower, crisp, and a carnelian moon,
Two feathers touching brush her cares away

Also an involved sea shell she keeps
In her silver box, at least
So she says, but
That's about all – my voice
Escapes for singing and my eyes you said
Go misty when you say a thing to excite me, sad
Or happy

In Anatolia

Slit eye, so young, in your place,
I mean no harm, but see you
And am close, in this light, so
Close. Food, knives, a red floor peak
And are gone in your flesh glow. The curve
Of a bird comes back to me.

Yes, it was big, as birds go. Blue wings,
A throat, I think, rain-rose, and a crest.
All at once it flew out of no place.
It perched on a plinth of white stone
To flute the one song it knew.

Noon: heat in this old town spent
Long breaths on rock. Wells dry. A few
Cubes of shade. Candid weeds made sure
The song could last. Pure notes
Go well with dust; in the doom of that high place
Time showed its drift.

On that plinth it put down claws, a bird,
Spikes – it told the air
What it meant: *io dio*, it sang. *Io dio*.

You will not say it. Your hair is
Coiffed to fall, soft, across your face,
As if your face should not be shown here –

A wing, gloss, when
You shake your head like that you hide
Most, at least, of your face. Wax
Boys, they sit, one by one, dumb, with hands
They fold and twist, here, at this feast:
You do not foot their bill.

Rich you might be, or
Not, but are you here? Your place seems
Close to oak boards, wild rice, raw fish.
That blue bird, you are with it.
Still you have ways to resist
Dead mouths, our small norms, blood that froze,

So much heart ache. Why, white stones
Once were grooved, to hold up roofs. White
Stone, fierce hands hewed it
Into forms. Through the fresh
Stone robes a god flew, those days, a pulse
It was thought. Worse off by far,
We have none or put ours in the wrong place.

Stand there and speak. Tell
Why no springs flow there. Why no folks walk
The old streets. Did the no-good bird
Eat the gods up? Let your wing fall
To hide your face. We do not know
What now to fear most.

Pink Slippers

Pink slippers –
The voices
Return, the voices
From Antioch, Agrigentum, wherever
Return, clear

Splitting apart
The bottled, rotten
Remnant we
Dwell in, with a swish
Of clothes falling

From limbs radiant
The voices
Return. She stood
And shook
Off everything, stood

In the silver light
A moment,
In a forest, in
A city, ancient lamps
Marble paving –

And the pink
Slippers? Later they
Crossed
A road, other feet
Than hers in them,

But to death
He loved them. Pink
And voices, distinctly
They spoke, delivering the drift
Of old stories –

Wickedly
The swish, the dark
And silver joy, the arms
Holding, the perfect
Fit, immediate

Another Village

− Atmosphere
Wrong: past noon a sunlight
Denser than flesh, across
A bowl of red

Berries women at the
Marbletop
Table
Softly talking −

And the wild, fingery
Garlic flanks
The ravine, apricots
Quicken to be bitten −

Old bell, one chime
Remote − wind down deeper
Ruffling vine leaves;
Muscular,

Gorged with heat
A pine cone prepares
To open, crack, the poplar
Shivering − bluer, there

And now a mountain
Lifts, the idiot
Framing a theme can
Sit up and write about it

The Shape

Funny, you keep it to yourself. Not quite:
Scraps of the story escape, take on
A runaway life of their own. Funny
It has to be hurt so, hurt so, still.
Draw breath, deep, breathe again, if you can.

Waking in a blinded room, improvising a vision
For her: dawn breaks over a brigantine,
From Patras to Palermo. Listen to the sea.
Mystery Greeks, bottles of ouzo, scent of pine.
This wheeze (it has to be) of an accordion.

Or worshipping one curl, all of a piece with her.
Had anyone noticed it? No, nobody before.
One touch and the cusp unfurls to cling
Close to an ear. It had to mean no less than love,
Perfect in sunlight, more than one half-afternoon.

Now it's nothing, nothing at all, she says.
Drunk as owls the sailors dropped asleep.
What is that faint plume on the horizon,
Not even marking the repeatable sea?
The curl persists, another where the lips

Of her sex meet. But she took off, that was it.
Forest thickens, torn you roll in it alone.
The room, sunken, waits for an oak to grow,
Fresh planks, to house again the shape
That shelters what escapes for it is certain.

Relic

Powdered wood from a beam
And plaster from the ceiling
Sift into dunes among the random
Worm-holes peppering my desk.

Overhead the flying machines
Buzz, on their occasions. I admire
The hood worn by the lime tree;
Scent of its flowers, I breathe it in.

They cluster in threes or fours, like bells;
Bees in the hood and scarabs hum;
The bird with a black mask stops to listen,
Spidery claw on a flagstone.

I am wondering at the fluency of its lines,
And how the tail flits, when all at once,
At the top of the winding stair,
You stand in a torrent of light,

Dressed in silver linen, as you wave,
Hatless, ready to go, your sleeve
Uncaptured, a spray of flower bells
Tilting across the tassel of your parasol.

Rilke's Feet

1

Heart bowels hand head and O the breast
So many of the parts fan out
Pressing on speech
Each a shape distinct
At length delivered a message
Classified sensitive

2

Perched in my tree as the light
Tries to unfold over Wilmersdorf

Rilke's feet a phrase
Ran amok in the mass below –

But in the grass
Not a trace left – playing

Woodland god he walked there
Barefoot – before architecture

Boiled the green to stone gray –
1897: I had taken my shoes off...

3

Sweetheart, Lou

... what is God, Mama?

                    "White hinds
                hidden in a thorn thicket"

No compliment to the long
Undulant chevelure of Magdalen

On a billow of mud
            in the Dordogne or Ariège was it
A footmark printed
            lightly
Hard mud in a deep cave

Might last another 15,000 years

But Rilke's feet
                he left them
                            standing
To be invented

4

This hot pursuant of
The Incomparable

A sort of hassock stool
He kept and kneeling on

Upholstered velvet
Worshipped any woman

He had invited no
Not any but this

Was the way he tended
Kneeling on the stool

And gazing up as
She waved an arm or

Cringed and bit her lip
Footless for some quaint

Antiphallocratic reason he
Poised at hers

A projectile
In a catapult

5

Or Rilke had no feet at all
What he had was fins
Up he twiddles into the air

Sycamore seed going the wrong way
Lands in my tree
Owl's eyes large liquid

Blink at me   Contrariwise
He had no body just a head
Thought a little girl

No body in his clean but threadbare
Clothes crossed the room
And took a cake with Mama later

Off again
Somehow bowing
Where can he have put that cake?

6

More famous feet
Than these invisible ones
The foot of Philoctet-
Es and Byron's

186

Hoof with its iambic knock
On the deck of a gondola,
Incidentally – copper,
His horse adored the hot

Weight of it and ladies
Lifted fingers to their eyes,
Thrilling stomachs
Fancy the surprise

Suddenly milord is dead
While muttering Greek
Bandits around his bed
Frenetically seek

To screw the damn thing off,
Here's Philoctetes' foot
Festering in a cave –
His wound minute by minute

Throbs away the years,
Four thousand of them spin
Till Troy falls to hexameters
And Rilke's feet begin

7

A Wicked One
When he scraped the Many
Bits together
Must have made some funny faces

Rilke's feet – how
Is this body
To be looked upon: a

Screen or
Not sure a
Scene a recipient interim

187

And liminally
In and over it creation's
Wavering shapes break open
Yet

Are distorted it is
The dance but done
As if by hangmen

Touch and look
From a footsole run
Tightrope lines to every single organ

8

Voice where are you now
Tree what has become of you
Never a column or pedestal
But a tree of branching blood vessels
A tree trying to speak
Through thunderous pumping of juices
I climb across this voice
In the grip of its twig deletions

9

Hands whose touch is thinking
        How the taste of orange flows
To the beat of a ringdance

Slowly out of its givens
        The automatic body
Builds itself

Might balance feet with
        Strong straight
Articulations but dammit

An orchestra of echoes
    Code of interchanging
Trait and ancestor

All we can see in one photo
    Is Rilke in
Well shone shoes with spats

Its constant monologue
    Broken by torture
Reroutes no signals

And a shoe might hide
    One discord perhaps a hand
Froze an insurgent impulse

And clogs
    In the negative
I am told

Now like an undesired
    Eyeball captive in a pod of skin
For fingers wished it

Footward as a pipesmoker
    Tamps tobacco
Down to the base of the pipe bowl

So blue huggermugger knobs
    When bones obtrude strum on tendons
Fuming toes

Recoil to plot
    Inversion of the message
Train to be fingers and pluck back

Their slice of the power
    Did Rilke then support a claw
Brain-limb feedback

Did it flush his touch of sphinx
    Faintly at the tip
With repression's rose

189

Rilke's feet
Wading in a weird
Kettle of fish

The lobster
Has gone for a walk
With his ghost
The sea
Once
Too often

Xenophon Xenophon it were fit to include
Dark as it is again in Wilmersdorf
An echo of your script from Corinth, your
Fictional grammar of the human foot

Anabasis uh I am tired and my secret
Reader wonders where we have got
As did your mob of Greeks thirty years before
Thirty years before you finally wrote

A bit boastfully about the march to the sea
Then how your lines inch by inch
Barrelled along the barbarous coast

But hardly anyone cares now
About the fleetfooted Carduchi
Peltists and bowmen coming up quick

When they shoot they put the left foot out
And rest the base of the bow on it
Drawing back the string

You must have stopped to see that

And soon backwards the snow
Is opening its white tomb

Illshod columns of infantry
Straggle into Armenian mountains
Was there no shit they could not bite through

Newly flayed oxenskin
Froze that night to the footsoles
Thongs cut into ankle flesh

Many perished
Snowblind thwacking spear on shield
Throat racket body racket made the foe
Feel outnumbered

Small bags later we tied
To the horse hooves else
In the snow to their bellies they sank

12

Can I speak to you now Rilke
As we sleep
A little for our lives
Though I wonder sometimes what you meant
And my memory is awful
The footloose motions you enact or track

In poems where the verbs
Amaze by their precision
Were you pointing
Beyond the combative body which engulfs
All as nothing with its bubble

Pointing to a body more like music
A luminous relator with its warmth
"Transfiguring the earth"
If it was this what have we got
Not evil quite wondrous desires
But injustice

It may be too late
Your invisible

Feet can do nothing but insist
Issue into a space all
Rondure and volume void

Of anything more dense
Than the thrum of air you felt
Around a seagull's wing
As it poured the pearliness in
And fitted feathers

Threadless motion
Through it your truant feet
Sprinkling punctures might
Sustain
Like intervals between them utterly

Determined throngs of stars
Or freely quickening and distinct
These feet it is
That ease
The gasps of joy from children's throats

Quasizeros

21 MISCELLANEOUS MICRO-POEMS
for Hans Vogt

1

Walking, stopping in
Mid-stride

Leaning on air, word on the tip
Of the tongue

2

In the creases of her finger pointing up
To stress not that, but this, what

192

Else but

Eloquent miniscule
Horizons of grime

3

Watch the velvet
Black
Big
Birdspider piano
Finger his moonlight
Sonata, eight arpeggios
To cross
Your bed

4

All the limbs
But not a stitch

Stretched, then, in their folding, that
Much the more naked

5

Level head, one hundred such,
Hardly to be seen, tilted

Imperceptibly forward, and
If cocked

Not predatory, never a
Mountain top mistily

Bloodying the dreams in it,
Might, no, not even

These might have rectified
The nasty bent

Our species took, ignorant
From desire, gungho with dread

6

Slow wings beating take
Motion from unharmed air

Around children who break at sunrise
Bread and will not grow old

7

                    Possum breath
– whiff of the One
            Tongue?
                Imagination –

Heard a mouth
            open
                    Looked for unicorn (cornered
mirrors) by

Flashlight a ratlike
                baldish creature
Weaving

                    Through fresh bark mulch
Pellets, in distant
                Indigo, still driven

To pick among the
        Crusty spitball
                        Subterrene (*Nastürmchen!*)
Nasturtium seeds

8

Frowned –

So droopingly
The roof

Tiles overhead
– Heavy

Red beef

9

Hellbent, thunderstruck
Piss-asses, locust men
Grope for popcorn, nip the beercan

Gape at a screen

Face cooked
In a helmet
Stole the show for one

10

Head thrown back
Feet skimming the ground, who

Is this coming so fast she's
Lost from sight?

11

Scorched wizard
Sloped indoors, heard his babies

– A Squelch of organs – uncorked
A bottle of Ghost,

Ate his Lantern, slept, in his high
Horse head, catastrophic, nought

But song of a katydid:
Darkening a mountain, shaking out

The hair of the world

12

God, pining for whom helps
Keep some slim

Strip from this, pray, tormented
Skeleton the wobbling

Fat rolls that make him speak
Instead of thunder, with a squeak

13

Heavy logistical weapons of muscle mass rush
Up front to fling
A stone

                    Hated squirrel
                 Gulps another mouth-
                    Ful of bird-

                              Seed frisks
High / lightly   His tail
                              Melts into the trees

14

Not the eyebrow, its
Traject, not the gorgon

Hairmass, lady,
What is it, this

Mirrorless me
Topples them

Cracking, somehow
Into your pit?

                    15

Cuff tucked
Back, palms up to

Help you squinny at
Her cuts

                    16

A gartered swinger in the human tree
Enjoys her husbands to the tune of three

Her flesh still willing when they hit the floor
She signals for a half half dozen more

Those being spent, her art not stopped, she swings
Up, to catch her breath, her heart on other things

                    17

Glossy, not from clinging, these
Knuckles predecease her quilt –

Eyelid sliding back peels a white,
Now she called a name, joyfully, it was mine

But in the country she came from
Girls divined their fortunes

In shapes of wax they sprinkled hot,
At random, over water

                    197

18

Dry smell, dark yellow
   tugs at heart thongs –
old leatherbound books, bays glow,
   drifting
when first light stirs up
   the pure fume

19

With cabbage
Leaf ears
Pinned back and young
Stumbling elephant steps I ran
Up to you,
Poetry, but almost
You had forgotten

Me, you
Gave me a lick,
Delicate and
Suspicious, the way
A lion, lowering
His tongue,
Drinks

20

        Hollering into the
    Pool
A wild
   Peony of boys
       Lobs its petals

21

As limestone through smoke
   goes amber
     so goes the world

Through my slit eyes, clenched
hands, when I
write these poems

A Pinwheel

In his luggage X had stowed a green
Bronze arrowhead. The thing
Came from Armenia, Persian, he said.
Successive satraps in its time
Had all the best Armenian horses herded
South to the Persian king,
Rugs, tubs of turpentine, oil in jars,
Boys tactfully picked –

                On the mantelpiece
Y had a stemmed
Wooden cup from Crete. A convict
Made it. You might think
Fingernails not a knife had oddly
Whittled its
Maze of facets, groping for the tilt
It had to stand at. Piss gold the colour
That man's privation wept
And sorrow sweated into it –

                Since 1940, Z
Has kept a coin, Macedonian. Curly head
Of Zeus on one side. Philip II
Leans forward, if you turn it, on a high
Stepping horse. Silver tunic still
Flutters around his body.
Silver hat brim twisting in the wind –
Years to go before the drink got him
Or bugles blew, at crack of dawn, and Alexander
Floated off, unblinking, in a cloud of archers.

A Different Banquo

for Alberto de Lacerda

A ghost speech
I bring you, with my voice.
When you have gone, my voice will be forgotten.

Ghost speech I
Said, friends. But it's not quite
So far along. Here we are, if still we are

Not yet dead,
Nor gaga. True, any
Moment, any, could for ever extinguish,

Think of it,
The wave. So I ask you:
Remember things I said for fun, not insult,

Even when
Your ears, I said – they're big,
Can you wag them? Or: your lisp kissed sawdust. That

Little mole
On the tip of your nose –
A beacon? Could it guide through storm a long ship?

Can you switch
It off? Does it send up
Punctual signals? Intrusive things like that

I said. In
Hope you'd be provoked. In
Fear a soul might then respond, giving me back

Tenfold the
Joy it was to be there,
Humbly, with you, facing you, in natural

Light. The crust
Of this planet under
Us. Or yawning through our reckless candle flames

The abyss,
Unaccountable. To
Your memory admit me and my weird jokes;

The help I
Ever was to you need
Be no further concern. Still, hold against me

Failings, or
Possibly pettiness
I showed at times when talk ran wild, was too grand

– When you die,
I said, Lord, you'll say, back
I come now, but he'd never known you were gone –

For a voice
Can be wrenching, can pluck
Out of a sky the moon, full, mute, properly

Blent with it.
Yet will you raise me up
Again, at your feasts? Also in lonely rooms

Which exist?
Drink whole flasks of me, raw
Red wine, never negligent? Give me a chance.

As for what
I wrote – thumb through it on
Weekdays, and skip, if you will, the rotten bits.

Or else, by
And large, have done with it.
Save your breath to resist contenders, who kill;

Cruel pack
Rats, they are organized,
And horror has no end. Acquiescent, I

Cried out, but
The soul in that sound was
Gashed by evil's claw. Heart now full, vacant soon,

At the beck
And call, leastways, of drab
Manipulators, don't we all bide our time?

Little mouse,
With your voice now I shriek,
So small I made myself, hoping to slip through

Power's mesh.
Not good enough. I had
Chosen to be trapped. To be free was far too much

Breath wasted.
So greed abolishes
Good things, and the canny have no place to go:

Thus we loved,
We did, wildly, trusting
One passion. For, divisible, we only

Loved one voice,
Soaring, not mine. It comes
From the sky, weeps, laughs, shakes into shape our trees.

Richard Lion Heart

His country, what a place to have lived in:
Farm girls bringing milk for free, taste of berries,
Sunshine all summer long, the salmon leaping,
Snow crisp in winter, smoke from cottage fires.

I'll ride beside my king on horseback,
Rock hard river valleys hear him sing:
His new song in langue d'Oc for the redbreasts
Goes to the tune of silver horsetails flicking.

In time a wise anarchy will be possible.
Bursts of laughter have washed away oppression,
If anyone wants to govern, gracious people do.
He'll cure my wart and I will clean his crown.

No whining nasal voices, no la-di-da,
No craving for empire, no rotting industries;
Village ponds and words and coastlines are unscummed,
No scummy timid souls could haunt that England.

In Byzantium we'll booze it up, feast with friends
In the south of France. Ah, didn't they clap him
Into a dungeon? I'll spring him. Past far timberlines
We'll clatter on mules and ask the way to Japan.

Lento

To be almost unable to wake up
To see the shadow of a spider's web
To be interested in it sleepily

To notice that the shadow is active
To wonder about its reiterated movement
To think its movement varies from time to time

To call it ocean
To feel it living in the room
To lie full length in the golden light the room contains

To hear the clatter of plates in the courtyard
To forget the shadow of the spider's web
To open the door and approach the plates

To feel hunger
To recognize that your hunger is privileged
To raise your arms

To take a knife in one hand
To take in the other hand a fork
To consider the veins in the marble table top

To admire on your plate a grilled ocean
To eat a helping of spider pie
To taste the white infinitive wine

The Mol

There is a mol and in a lake
She said he lives
And how he sleeps
How deep the water is
How cold and dark

Boatmen shiver and the mol
Lifts his mouth like this
She imitated it
Her jaw flew out an inch
She snapped at nothing

There he is and once a rope
Weighted with a stone
They lowered it for miles
Something tugged at it
They pulled it up she said

The rope was bitten off
The stone had gone
They tried a chain
The chain went down and down
The chain was bitten off

She said he doesn't hurt
He only wants to sleep
The mol is gentle yes
He goes like this
A mouth (I thought) we feed

Halicarnassian Ghost Dialogue

What can the old fool have been looking for?
Back there we had the Many in the One.
If he looked back, this is what he saw:
A ridge, a contour, stark, like an eyelid,
Framing a shrub or two. Barefoot
A little girl, where the lane lofts its dust,
Dragging branches back to a hovel.

He never saw her. If he heard
The heaven bird warble in the pines
And the wind foreveraftering, still
On he went,
Not anxious that his donkey might break down,
There'd always be another; but he hugged
A secret such a fool knows nothing of.

As in a dream a man's thought swings
Many ways between his times, touching
Past and present, hangs between
Dithering signs that sparkle in the vault
Of his flesh, and others, buoyant, yet
More dim, pained, and these
Exact a meaning from him, they propose
To be restored, whole, put back beyond
His death, their origin, the one thing
He never will have known – so he swung
Out, and capably

The donkey trotted under him, unaware
Of all the torchlit cities, fumes, of horns,
Remote, and ceremonies, deaf to voices
That reeked or howled or sang
Sayso into his cranium

It was the story
Of a girl with a branch, you might say;
Of a hill, stark, contour
Framing sage and oleander. How come,
Everything was changed? He alone
Could sit in the cool and figure, not afraid,
Pen in hand, the monstrous variables,
Plotting their tracks.

The air, this
Excited us all. None but a few
Did anything about it. A rose, a white
Pebble, look good; at nightfall, in the mouth
A taste of olive. Nothing was enough
To make much palaver about. Wounds, quivering,
Suck the world into their vacuum, when –

When curiosity like his whets its hook
On the air between impulse and action.

There was no story till he tugged
The atoms together.
                          Not only for his own good
Does a man pan from dust a glint
Of original information. Spinnackers
Of oddity, majestic
The ripple of ideas, these, our thread,
Irreducible amalgam of our discourse,
He combed from the gabble of old salts,
Horsemen, crones, bandits.

                          Listen, was it
His feeling that any heap
Of rags, palpitating on a roadside,
By a tethered goat, or roping hay
Into a sack, has something to speak of;
That any individual is ringed
By a glowing exoskeleton, the tissue
Of stories and of dreams it craves to tell?

And his eye magnified it into a folly of wands,
Ligatures, with pennons cracking,
Cones, strained pulleys, psyche
Thinging itself into an essential
Funniness, a pupa, something
Like birdsong, or
A ship of resistance, and of wonder
An instrument. No one girl
Who drags her branch down a lane
Matches any other.

                          This exciting air, this
Time, this phenomenal
Melting skin,
        chrysalis of inventions, thickened
With sorrow, so he imagined it,
With such zest – no choice, but to display,
He forced it to, colour, with strangeness.
He loved it so, stripped

Or like a woman who walks, walks
As a tree might, or a fountain at daybreak,
Unfathomable.

Was he saying that home, after all,
Depends on the difference you make of it;
Wild, like a sheen; in a heron's eye,
Pigment? Any domain
Warms to delight, hopelessly fragile,
When someone sets a rose,
Fresh, in the middle of a dinner table.

No. He was saying that this little girl
Was born alone, lived alone, dies alone.

An Old Wine Press

1

An old wine press
With its iron screw
Column down the middle –
Vertical slats doubly hooped
Contain the tub – this instrument
Sepia on account of its being
Not the very thing but a photo dated
No later than 1910

2

Higher up, steep slant of a barn roof.
The line of its eave like a lip,
Wavy. A sort of monster
Grin goofily reveals
The stubs of seven teeth, unless
These are beam ends or swallows' nests

3

And halfway up the slant
Two holes are built, like little eyes, or else
They breathe for the hayloft, handy
Homes of dove, dark lodges
For the grape scented air

4

All this no more than a glimpse
But the barn behind the wine press caught
And carries onward
A human imprint, rough hewn
A flicker of the torch

5

Here for once
Doubly precious, considering these
Eight people grouped around the press:
Just a bunch of farm folk, three generations,
The men clothed in stained denims, sweaty caps;
The woman has pinned a flower to her breast
And holds an empty cheese basket;
A little boy had curled his fingers
Around the handle of a hooped
Wooden wine jug

6

There they stood, tilting
Every which way; splay feet, beefy arms
Dovetailed into a right good
Angular design:

Three men
Lean against the tub on its platform;
If this beard might crumple into a king's mask,
Still clog and boot crack with mud
And glue these
Dancers to the ground; the boy
Hangs in the middle, perched, dangling
Tiny booted feet –

Any moment
The glass he grips by the stem will spill;
Oddly tender yet, the way
All around him thicker fingers hold
The scarce seen cool substance –
In it gleams the god, red and savage,
Spinning the world for more than money

7

Yet the money matters. You can plot
Grim pursuit of it in the skew
Cheek folds of the white-haired man.
Hope made the woman's mouth
A thin long line and in her round chin
Totted up
Credits of hair, winnings of eye, decimals
Of nostril

8

Who knows, it is mostly too late;
The wine that time at least
Had a fair chance;
The footwear might see another ten years out,
As good as a second skin, these denims
Are worn as the sun
Wears its light, or as the god they nourish
Squid-wickedly has thrown
History over his tentacles, a robe
Smoky in colour, a tissue of bloodstains,
Whose, fading, sepia

Irish

Here as the bamboo
leaf and rod
glisten
in broken moonlight
this harp music

I suppose it echoes
the strings of rain, silver
those dark pools
drink up
on streets in Ireland

Say time could have taken
a different shape,
but this, with red eyes that weep
and search the horizon
choose we did

Say a spirit got
knotted
in spilt intestines, a body
of music shattering
the bamboo door

Now leaf and rod
the fawn I saw stopped
in a clearing, pulsars in moth-
eaten velvet
flash slow beacons

But a perception chosen
digs historic
claws deep down, not
like the bamboo rhizomes
they touch dancing

Pickled
in this whiskey bottle was
a heart, do not listen
the wind sings in its
ventricle, seaward

Cabaret de la Canne, January 1855

Sir, I do not know your name,
Nor do you know mine. So we sit,
Briefly, at neighbouring tables, you
With your bottle, the cat on your knee,
I with my little glass.

In our sunken ship
The third table has been taken
By the fine man of darkness, whom
We do not see. Look, on the furrowed surface
Glittering still, the flake of snow I flicked
From the collar of my coat when I came in.

Each sits watching
The face of his own slowly turning
Universe. Particularly the cat
Has known how the heat
Comes and goes. Important smells
Wrinkle and flex into signatures, you know,
Writ small in snowflakes and the skeletons
Of leaves. Shuddering,
The fingers of a spirit ink into our skins
Mysterious names, numbers, and messages.

Ancient gutters
Accommodate the cat, providing
Fish, spare ribs, a scrap of lamplight;
Spilt milk to lap up, now and then.

There are places where people turn yellow,
Having nothing to eat. Cloacas, attics.
Broken roofs. Through holes the snow sifts.
A Valois song can be issuing, in another street,
From a little girl's lips
For a penny.

Mandolins, a lantern swaying, make it
Difficult to want less than a tree to dance with.
Do we suffer
Most because the bunched worms will hang

211

In the emptiness you are looking at, this
Dome of mine, bald, this bony cabin?
                    What is immortal
If not the injustice?

There was a room I lived in once,
I remember how the early light in it
Fell across two rescued Fragonards.
There was a girl, nearly naked she was,
Tigers ran before her on a leash
And a little donkey woke us, braying,
Or a barge trumpet's echo off the river.

Like a swift in his globe of crisp mud
I hung between sleep and waking
And heard the straw speak in my thin
Mattress. Look, here it is, another face
Of that same
Towering light, again
In this bit of a rainbow, at its peril
Afloat in the eau-de-vie:
I drink it for the dream that spills
Into life.

They tore it down, it was an old house.
They did not tear down
The other room, which, if you follow me,
We put there, suspending it
Outside any space that iron balls
Can shatter.

In that room the last vine still grew,
A veiny green, very ancient.
The last vine, first planted when
The emperor was Julian and Paris Egypt.
From the vine,
Yes from it you might see
A light as from the original stars unfolded

And flew as it pleased, to vary
As it touched the featured walls through
Twelve emotions. With snaky lines

212

It marbled the stones and old chairs
We had broken by leaning back to laugh.
To eye the stones was to feel a flow
Of female warmths and hear the goddess, –
Moan and shriek of the sistron in her fingers.

What can you be thinking?
No, do not indispose the cat.

Rosenkavalier Express

Sundown in the dining car of the Rosenkavalier Express –
   I am seeing the packed trees and fields of wheat,
Dense greens involved with depths of indigo,
   For the sun – all day it shone like nobody's business,
And I think that a poem should be like these
   Packed trees and wheat, a tuft aglow, an indigo thing;
Then for a split instant I'm happy, a thrill goes through me,
   The dinner of beef and wine, shock of a salty
Taste in the beef, the red ordinary wine,
   Might account for it, but robuster than any reason,
Visceral or not, is the briskness of it, I mean
   The spasm, spliced with a sweet twinge of doubt
Whether I'd ever be up to voicing a poem like that.

And there was the whole day sunlit in Vienna,
Hungover a bit after hours of drink with friends;
   I am still out on a walk at one in the morning,
The big idea was to find, at last, the Mikado,
   But I couldn't, so now I'll never be sure
If a special whore called Josephine hangs out there.
   I am still strolling around at one in the morning
Though it is eight p.m. and as the train swings
   Westward into the night, fields will be warm as beds,
A peace envelops me from eyebrow to anklebone,
   I want to say thank you to someone for letting me
Eat and drink and feel on my flesh, whizzing by,
   These tufts of pine, these depths of indigo,
Rhombs of wheat that surge in the wind;

Birds and rabbits will be rustling through them,
Smells drift, sprung by sun from June rain,
    Prickly smells of wing and fur, rose and lettuce,
Search in me for the tautest bowstring, holding
    But lightly holding the midpoint of the bow.

Ah well, the Mikado stroll was a washout,
    But with coffee there comes a little sugar packet
With "Mikado" printed on it, and a gasp, childish
    Enough – I catch my breath as the large
Rhythm of coincidence wraps me in a fold of fire.

    What is this? Moneyless but sometimes lucky
I have been ways with women that made them powderkegs.
    Wrong, time and again, I have wounded people,
Fallen short of their dreams, risen to them
    Too little or too late; less and less I can tell
What feeling is good for, but have been acquainted
    With animals fierce and beautiful, so to whom,
To what should I give thanks, and thanks for what?

    What have I brought to love, if not catastrophe?
Now ideas flock like moonsheep in my turning head,
    Now I see roof angles, wooden cabins in cabbage plots,
Goalposts and staircases, and so rotund a hill,
    O, distance slips into its blue mist, but point blank
Stalks of wheat and blades of grass freshen again.
    As if through me Imagination wanted, sightless,
To fondle the volumes of objects and read their legends,
    Trim old barns and now the Danube, full stretch,
Open lips that motion to speak, wag their tongues.

    So I think of the tongue of a blackbird,
And that I won't call this moody aria "Mitteleuropa."
    Grateful not to be dead, or frightened, or oppressed,
I think of the call in the song of a blackbird:
    When you patrol the dust of Mitteleuropa
It doesn't perceive that you and history are there;
    It sings with a voice that must be dreaming
It is a petal and so, rosily, all for free,
    In one cool fold of fire the petal wraps you.

Local Roads

These local roads they say
In Texas hug their curves
Or cracks and hollows
Like ancient pain

I looked ahead
I thought a turtle or what else
A flexing clump a shell
Had waddled half across

I ran to find if I was wrong
But there it was
Again the vacant womb
A god imagined human music from

My impulse the reverse
I slipped that hood back on
I shrank into the shell
To shield a scaly head

Whirled into the air I heard
Colossal whistling shoes
And fingers beating time
But vaguely on my back

Caught up with me at last
What century was this
My negligible weight
How balanced in his hand

Scars of ancient lightning
Scollop the vaulted shell
What if they broke open
What frenzy would he feel

Driving Home

Imagine you might forget
The white road
Splitting away from the black road

Not loaded words

Imagine you
Might forget its whiteness and
In the identical moonlight

A different smell of burnt cedar

But it was never white was it
A gray blue gone to violet rumpled
Like denims in a surplus store
White road – pulverized

Limestone bathed in the rays

You might forget the fork imagine
Sound of the owl further down the road
Splitting your time
Between now and the hearing of it

A voice inappositely pink
O whiskered shrimpish owl

But then you never forgot
Pursuing the tubes of light
How it felt

More like a branching tree than a church
Made ghostlier
By the fact of a candle in it

Never so new
It was not to be afraid

Imagine
Talking and happy stripped
Inside not even shutting the door
The forgotten embrace

Now when you came together
It will nourish
All the ways everything moves

A Portrait of J.L.M.

We called him spirit of the place,
But he's more like a good old tree root.
Went off, a year gone, back to Rockport.
It seems, when he'd gone, us not even
Knowing it, everything fell apart.

             Wish I remembered
What he told me. This bit of town I landed in,
These railroad tracks he'd known, secret
Signs chalked on the freight wagon doors,
Hobos bivouacking, and how he'd drift across,
Talk with them. That was far back
In the Thirties, near enough to the yard on Seventh
He got our big old bamboo from, planted it.

             Wanderings, the split rail
Fences he built, him wiry then as now, bird faced,
Out west of Sanantone; any job he could find
He put both hands to. He belonged with
Boilers of big ships, blue clouds
Of working people on the move, tumbleweed;
You do the most you can.

             Far out hereabouts
He'd gone courting, before big money
Rolled the roads in. Remember now,
Hummed the tune once, he did. They walked out

Through live oaks together, rocks, and cedar,
Listening to the trickle of the creek in Spring.
He sat his Mildred down, kissed her,
Same old tune in their heads.

        I ate her cakes
She'd later bring at Christmas down the hill,
Stopping to chat a while, propped against
The doorpost, she'd laugh like anything
But sometimes she took ill.

        Drains, spigots, carburettors,
The pump, I saw his knuckles whiten
When he fixed them, and later his hand
Shook, breath caught, and as he worked
His mouth helped, with twists and lippings.

        Rolled his own cigarettes; told me –
Here's this old song book, found it at the county dump,
You want it? 1865 – Irish songs. Irish
As his Indian scout grandfather had been. He'd
Told him of hilltops hereabouts

        Where the Indians hunkered,
Yawning. And how a coach might rumble by,
Gold or guns in it, stuff they could use. And how
Into this cave his grandfather went once, deep,
Now they've blocked it, but it goes underground
All the way from the lake to Tarrytown.
A volcano, too, he said
        I might not believe it,
Not so far off, east, he found obsidian there,
Beyond where the highrise banks and turnpikes
And the military airport are. Trees,
He loved trees and drove miles to see them
At their best, the right time of the year.
Buckeye and catalpa in their first flower,
Chinaberry, dogwood.

        All birds had ordinary names,
Like redbird, but once in a while he'd speak
Old words, not from books but from Tennessee,

Like once he said "quietus." Always
Flesh in his words, and bone, and in his doings,
Not absent even from the way he'd knock
A bourbon back, straight, that was the way
He liked it, then roll another cigarette.

               For Mildred when her teeth
Fell out he whittled deer horn so she'd have
A biting edge up front. When he came by, dressed
Smart for a visit, he'd be wearing false
Rat teeth up front and give a wicked grin.
There was this park he kept,

               He knew all the weeds in it,
All, and told how some weed sent
Cows mad and was taken too much liberty with
By them young folks as went out there
For a high time.

               Well, then he'd push off
In his battered pickup, headed for a honkytonk
Some place down the line. Why don't folks look at
That kind of man? Some say insight
Comes when you tell the individual
Get lost. What's all their deep droning talk
To him? He's too smart to think up
Revolutions, what's it, that perspective stuff?
Maybe he's nobody

               But he made things work,
Never slaving, nor ginrollizing. Made things
Shift and level with every breath he drew.
Had no grievance, spoke no ill of anyone
Or anything save spindly offshoots
Of tree roots that split drainpipes in the country,
Having ballooned in them, like brains
Got swole, so he'd say, with all the excrement.

Pinyon Incense

Oblong a pellet
In a small
Pueblo bowl

Careful
It could come to bits
A fleck like conscience

Burn as you light
One tip
And breathe on it a pang

Possibly a finger
Writing but
A fresh piece

And firm shoots mysterious blue
Scented smoke up
If ever the smoke thins

Look while ash
Blackens the tip it is
Not standing on

Down through the spirals move
Meet
Old man trombone brown

He stands
Where his feet keep him
At a cave opening

Watch the writ of furrows
Groove his dry
Pine bark

Palm he is
Not angry now he simply will not
Let you in

With your sorrow
And your bodyful of pacts
Broken

Let him say
Sorrow let him say
Nothing

Just cup like that his
Palm and cuff
The top of your head off

A Lyric to Stanley Myers' "Cavatina"

(in John Williams' guitar arrangement)

Blue cave, deep stream,
Stream, how you run;
Flow, clear, from the blue cave
For the sun to shine on.

Old sun, clear stream,
Not made for the pain;
Still you receive us,
Now and again.

High, high the falcon calls,
Mocks the world as he flies;
His shadow dips across the stream,
Silver, in the sunrise...

What means is not the end
But the movement of such things;
Watch the falcon move to the beat
And yielding of his wings.

Now there is this place, love,
Where we could belong –
A wave means to carry us
In the secret of a song.

Enough, enough that we flow
As often as we fly –
Not counting, old stream,
Time gone by.

A Young Horse

Where can it now have gone
The warm night ruffled
With screech owl feathers
Where can it have gone
When the horse came to a call

The warm night with branches
Haunt of moss web of intelligence
The breath of a young horse
Cooling between fingers
The night vast with bunched stars

Simply blown away it was
The night murderous and milky
The night of old hymns and hot bullets
Blown away by a breath
Curling between fingers

It flew between my ribs
It set a hollow throbbing
Between the ribs and fingers
A sort of pulse had shuttled
Felt as it wove and melting

Melting the shell this mortal
Man nocturnally hides in
His temple void of presence
With a wicket gate of muscle
To shield from shock his hungers

People in Kansas, 1910

1

Now they stand quite still on level doorsteps,
Outside the Drug Store and the Post Office.

A white sky, two buildings underneath it,
Outside the buildings half a dozen people.

Across the dust like dice the buildings rolled,
Stopped under the white sky.

Soon the people prised them open, clambered out.
Here at last. Here, they said, is Dorrance.

2

Stiff, like effigies, almost,
Made of language; speaking
The people came to be real for one another.

A head below the P of the Post Office
Shrinks into a Stetson. A wiry woman
Shoulders the stone Drug Store doorpost.

All six like effigies, wax, mechanical.
Work all day with corn, beans, soda pop.
The letters, few and far between. Senseless.

3

The people insist. But a vague terrain –
How can you fill it. Corn and letters
Stop short. The horizon,

A banker might one day darken it,
Locomotives. This big space frightens. We
Lost here a sense of belonging with the wind,

Now geese and trees that fly with it are no part of us.
Trust your shirt, these oblong blocks of stone.
Trust two dark heaps dropped in the dust by horses.

A chimney pot, back of the Post Office. Plain
Undistressed people, you never dreamed
Of burning letters, one by one, or bodies.

4

That's it. None could know what later crooked
Shapes
History takes when something radiant
All the brain and body cells cry out for
Is suppressed.

Behind bars appetites riot; captured
Guards
Sob for mercy; spies are fucked.
These oblong people lived out their free time
On credit,

They could count it wise not to wish
Their soap
Were sweeter, small business not
So methodical, dogs happy to work
Nights for them.

No. Their stark speech I do not understand.
Why
Make of life such a hard nut?
Or did they? Far off, faceless, kin of mine,
Hard living

Salt of the earth, sharply defined, crystal
Flakes,
You were never as oblong
As the buildings that warmed and warped you.
You weren't fooled.

Focus again,
So sharp you can smell the cigar,
The string beans taste
Just right. Objects, it
Was not your fault, objects, if
That is what you were, you have to go

Forth, shoulder your signs
In capital letters, onward to a place
I tell you of,
A place of blue and yellow. There
Mountains and people are one indivisible creature,
A grape admits night glow
To become its body,

Absolute, good as the bread
Is dense to the teeth
With death and legend. There, with patience
And the scent of sage,
People other than you ripened once
To a style – some to foreknow
And resist evil. Goodbye

Innocent oblongs, forget nothing
Now it is too late, but
Forget my fist with which if I could
I'd bang this postage stamp through
Into the reversed
World you stand in. It

Would stick in your sky of whiteness,
Perforated, a script of waves,
Muttering to you,
A voice, cancelled:
The sun does not shine for anyone,
The leaf arrives one breath
Only before the wind.

Minim

White owl over
Surface of a stream
No idea
What supports him

A Road that is One in Many

for George and Mary Oppen

This is a little road, this part of it
Like the centre bar of an old hand drill
Runs straight from this bend to the next

Hold tight when you walk along it
Violet orbs revolve under the pebbles,
Daily shadows. These vines have grapes

Shrub vines, bitter grapes, mustang. Hold tight
When this bird spider hauls his thick ass
Over the tarmac, this pothole is his

Hold tight to your straight walk, tiptoe
Certain spots are swept by heat
That is what blows, that is what dries

The inside of your mouth. The signs
Droop or rust, are not adequate
To the events they warn about. Warn

The pecan comes late into leaf, the big
Pecan; that is juniper, a cone, house
Of a singing bird. The signs do not sing

Being, but collisions, they take sometimes
A life or two. Hold tight, don't roll off, all
Sorts of people have walked along this road

This road is old, new, was Indian trail
By water, TU, they said, water; now
Corvettes and subarus, few foot people

This field in summer clings to a thatch
Of slow dragonflies; now nothing lives
In the tin shed, or is it nothing, only

Bugs, but you can moo to the ghosts
Of seven extinct preoccupying cows. Not
A slope in sight. These black

Eyed susans are the prettiest flower,
Later the dayflower marks its own distinct
Fluting off against this sky of skies

And the white rain, the white rain lilies
Really are these fragrant acid fruits
Of rain. Soon it stops. Under the polestar

At night hold tight still, grip this
Ground with your unshackled feet,
Don't scare these vines or ghosts are

Vines and ghosts. At night the lake
Is good for a swim. Don't mind these bats
That flit crisscross close to the cooling

Surface. Hold tight just once again,
Then let go and be consumed by the cool.
This is in the things and shines in the things.

Woden Dog

1

Wot doth woden dog
Por dog drageth plow

Thing odd dog not
Much good plow drager

But por dog drageth
All same plow

More come jellifish
Sting him woden dog

Jellifish in air now
Other odd thing

A speaking maner come
Round back to trooth

So doth dog plow
Plant seed of tree

Por dog life short
Woden dog long hope

Woden dog keep stung
Jellifish all round back

Dog hope tree grow
Much tree grow soon

Dog want find tree
Find releaf releaf

2

Bus drifer pleez
Make a smoth start
If not woden dog fall over

Bus drifer stop graduel
If not woden
Dog hit deck

Pleez bus drifer
Tern corner sofly
Woden dog cant hold on

You no he cant sit
Propper
You no he cant holtite

Forgoet how to life has he
Lest thing nock him sensles
All you no

Woden dog smoth graduel
Woden dog sofly he scare think
You forgoet how to drife

3

Jakit off jus warin sox like mean you
Woden dog reed times ever doggone day
Nites watchin his toob wow
Haffin the noose hapn

Wow fokes I tel you
Woden dog lap up noose
Woden dog bominate seecrit he reely do
Noose noose he bark runnin down street
Galumfin baknforth to his malebocks

He wannit so bad
He wannit to go
Like choclit maltn ketchup
Hole globe pakitchn pree paredn paid fur
Sitn in his noose baskit

No seecrit make woden dog
Bust out in flour one mawnin
Lookit soaps he buy woden dogfood
Killins toon that po looshn stuf
Brung home in his teeth

Come days wen he skratchn say
Mite try killin sumwun to make noose of me
Paps if I make noose off him
He dont done do it?

Woden dog howcom you loss
Yor own seecrit eye sunshine
Woden dog howsit taist that woden dogfood
Whars then kemel dog
Ever see canser wok a mile
Smokin up a kemel ever see war stop
Juscos you lookin?

Jeez fokes jus thort
If bad stuf stop no mor noose fur woden dog
Wot then ole flee bit dog
You see nuddin to lookat
You jus sit theren cry

4

Whodat
Striden backnforth in orifice
Who *dat*
Givin ordures

Whodat maken long biznis calls
Eatin long biznis bananas
He look horty
My whodat planifikting plitical fouture

Watchout
Here he come zoom by
Zoom silva jet clatter copta
Weekend in Toekyoe?
Meeting Younited Nayshun?

230

Whodat now
Widda dame in a yot wearin captin hat
Crakin lobsta
My my

Woden dog thats who
Woden dog how smart you done got

5

Hard inside
Woden dog

Woden dog gon
Sniff aroun for mudder

Mudder soft inside
Woden dog dig

Woden dog swetpant
Nuddin come up

No mudder
Dipressed woden dog

Dog shrink gifm pill
How that now help

Dog body keep movin
But inside he nut

No mudder inside
No soft strong mudder

Nuddin in world
Woden dog size

Howls too purty offen
In his dog house dum

So small he feel
Stinkin wikid woden

6

Yes derm dawg
Urmpteen snarls
Make nuddin
No bedder

You always countin
Countin crazy dawg
You mean
See me through glass

Derm yew lukn so glum
Like eny doods nuddin
Yew like like yew
Say dancein shit

Call yewsell a dawg
I aint buyin
Yew aint no morna
Cardbord ratlsnaik

Yew mean
Snarlin always makin
Fuss yew bossy think
Me mor stoopidn yew

Maybe too
But I countin
The timesnile git yew
Wunofem

Woden dog keep stil
So you can feel it
Movin

Rounanroun whirlin world
Why you keep with it
Is that reel

Woden dog
Keep stil so you
Can feel it movin

8

Hey now
Hoo done got hide
Inside you innerlekshuls

Meckin
Yore gin
Roll I say shuns

Hooz
Moovin yoohoo
All ways tokkin

Wokkin long
Rode like you wuz
Uh ginrollized creekin

Rekkernize hoo
He be my my if it aint are
Ole solom fren dubble you dee

9

Woden dog sittin
On the backstares

Sittin in the dark
Breathin a bit

What's this listen
Breathin

Laff
Woden dog

That's it
Laffin on the backstares

Thems wavesnwaves
Them cool backstares

Help dog floatin
Low float high

Not let waves go so
You seem zikazak

Doan it hurt some
Hey woden dog

Not let the laff hole up
In woden dog box

Listen breathin just so
Now no more done hurt

10

Wyso suddn everbody
Rite on walls

FREE WODEN DOG
Anifs time

Like I never got
Inclose free

Woden
Dog piksher?

Spose no place else
To rite

234

Silva smoak of pine
Burn chill
Woden dog shivver
Owl·not heard

Lightslice fix to floor
Think dead
Woden dog like ice
In his box owl not heard

Owl hoot rainbow
Out of owl eyes
Owl hoot rainbow wonder
Dog not see dog bark at ghost

Owl not heard
Dog munch heap white aple
Not feel snow as owl bountie
Not smell snow rainbow

Woden dog eat heap
Aple up
Pip corn all cold aple meat
Not see owl

Not see some owl eyes
Not hear
How pips look sound yum yum
Crunch owl eyes aple up

Dog wine in boxn stay putn scoff
Woden dog alltime scoff
Woden dog shut in wod
Not smell sweet pine

Woden dog not smell wind song
Burn swinging low
Swingin in pine wod
Owl not hoot fur him in pine log

Owl not hear in dog box
He woden dog
Snow owl hoot that rainbow now
Now hootn touch dog heart

After a Noise in the Street

It is the small
Distinct image, old as you like,
On a coin, or silvery
In a daguerreotype

Speaks to me:
The trooper Probus,
Two centimetres high, at most,
Helmeted, sloping

A spear
Across a shoulder,
Condenses all
The gas of empire

Into a few
Quick signs. No fuss, either,
Had perplexed her face,
This young and tawny

Woman, but
An anger, fine, makes
Luminous now the eyes
She levelled in Nebraska

At the lens, never
Exhausting it, for the hands
Folded and slender in her lap
Siphon a torrent

Of feeling through the image.
There is anguish
Untrapped, an ardent
Breath sets free to fall

A dew as on a cherry,
To magnify, by sharpening
So far, the resolute
Infinitesimal flesh, this wisp

Of being, only this
A mortal
Tentatively manifests. A
Measure just

One fraction grander could
Put back
Into the spear
Slaughter;

Distend a pleat
In this dress, or blow
A tassel up
Beyond belief – and it lumbers

Back into the flimflam; an
Embossed cuirass,
Probus any bigger, snagged
In power's mesh

Spills, as a blur, or boast,
His contracted time
Into the heaving
Primordial pettiness.

Hot Bamboo

My roots go
sideways
only
they
will
never
grope deep
nohow can
these
hollow
shafts
hold
remembrance
whenever
sounds
trickle
flute
gong
from
the crackpot's
pretend house
I
want you
moonlight
(if you
will)
to waft
them
over a touch
a merest whiff
will
send
me
responding
with a shiver
on my way
down
again
growing
to the hut

```
                    impossibly
                      a lake
                         is
                       there
                     an early
                       heron
                    suspended
                     in a mist
                        now
                      drinks
                       this
                       open
                        sky
                       limbs
                 of wild plum hide
                    old scrolled
                     mountain
                         so
                      spread
                       your
                        fan
                       soon
                      sighed
                     bamboo
```

Jerusalem, Jerusalem

White building under pecan tree
Four poles cradle the porch roof

Beyond gap in branches blue sky trackless
Shingle roof slope beckons ghost of pagoda

White wall veined with leaf shadow
Tree unfolds a boom of spray

Homely air, who knows which way moving
Tree pulse drums, cricket whistles tune

Old walls of wood creak when air cools
Tree spoke to folks indoors a rustling lingo

Crisp lettuce on their plates and red meat
Perched in tree same bird sang as now

Pecan tree sole hero still grows
Slowly war and work fetched those folks away

Too bad house now gone to seed
In trashed rooms white devils hang out

Tending itself – a tree in majesty
Glued to gum, soda pop, the white mouth

Look again: no thought can be too high
Of whisper locked in white heart

Tell thought: still harder time ahead
Don't hold against them drift of old song

Coral Snake

I had been planting the sliced seed potatoes
When the snake started up from underfoot
And slithered across the gravel I stood on.

His beauty was not the point.
He was the kind that kills in a minute or two –
Chop off the finger he bit, or else.
But he was beautiful: alternating the black,
Red, and yellow rings more regular far, thick or thin,
Than wedding bands on a jeweller's ringstick.

He had come out of nowhere like evil.
He didn't care about me or want me.
I cared about him enough – it was fear,

Fear, not for me, no, but for him, the snake:
Long-trapped, an old horror breaks loose,
Later you say Alas, the snake was beautiful.
So I wonder what I can kill him with,
And notice in my hand the hoe; he isn't far,
Full stretch in his ringed ripples I see him
Slithering east of the two asparagus ferns.

I whop the hoe down and nail his head in the gravel
Between the chicken wire fence and a vegetable frame.
But he won't let go, I'm wrong, his free head
Rose over the quartz and flint pebbles;
Wild, the taut pure body, to be moving on and on.

Nothing to be done; if I shift the hoe
He'll streak through the chicken wire and I'll be
Cut off. I pressed harder on the hoe blade,
His tough coil resisted and the head
Wove a figure of eight in a pocket of air.

I didn't want it to be done, I didn't.
But how now to stop, considering his pursuits,
Easygoing as he is, pinheaded, slow to bite –
They say his tooth sits so far back
He needs to chew to do you in.

For there was more snake now in me than him.
I pushed the hoe blade harder down
And reached around the gate post for a stone.
That stone I eased
Beneath his tiny weaving head, taunting him,
Then reached around the post for a second stone.

When I looked again
The small black head with its yellow nape band
Was pointing up and the mouth, opening, closing,
Snapped at air to repel the blind force
Which held him down.

I could not do it, not to him, looking so
True to himself, making his wisdom tell,
It shot through me quicker than his poison would:

The glory of his form, delicate organism,
Not small any more, but raw now, and cleaving,
Right there, to the bare bone of creation.

And so I gripped the second stone but steadily
Thumped that telling head down flat
Against the surface of the first stone.
The broken body, I lifted it up and dropped it
Later into a vacant honey jar. The colours
Now have faded; having no pure alcohol,
I pickled the snake in half a pint of gin.

Wild Flowers

Like voices
They never grew in water;
All began with nobody there to see.
A warmth helped; mud propelled them; early
The seeds rode in animal pelts across immense
Reeling distances, or
Were blown through light by the wind,
Like lovers.

When we were bush mice
They settled, ignored, in the cooling places;
Blood took heat,
Bees ate them, lizards and happily
Spiders like them. Lodged in the fat of horses
They travelled. Tigers, and us,
Still tree hoppers, hardly felt what colours
Ringed by unearthly
Fragrances without names they had.

Far off the glittering libraries,
Vases of blown glass;
But look,
On roadsides they exist. Songs in our hands
They go along with us. A passion
Means us to pick them, so

242

Responding to early light we stop; then drive on home
To draw blankets back
And make our love while sensing them,
Their far fields, their darknesses.

Dirge for the Mistress of Screaming Animals

Woke in the night
Amazing silence
Somewhere moon

Filling my hide out –
Milk, a truth –
Drank from a mirror

No sound in street
All systems muted
No buzz, no roar

No shout or shooting
Icebox, even
Forgot to hum

Ah but I longed
Solo in silence
For breath dream-quickened

A rustle beside me
Flesh on linen
Longed for her

Her scraps of sleep talk
Name she'd murmur
Said she worked

As a lab assistant
Chicks and rats
React to her shots

243

I see her stand
At the lab door heeding
Quick rat chatter

Her charts record
Behaviour graphs
In sign and figure

Why, mistress of
Screaming animals
Nevermore babble

Of mutable habits
Skills crepuscular
Hiding and seeking

Snap your fingers
Clatter a dish
Play me your heart beat

Give me your long shot
Fathom my sorrow
With your lost love cry

Bivouac

Among the Polish Chassidim, perhaps among the Chassidim
generally in Eastern Europe, it was prohibited to leave a
book open in the village reading room. A sacred book, that
is. Interfering forces might invade it, or escape from it.

A shadow might, otherwise, cross the open pages. The
shadow might distort the features of a divinity which inha-
bited the pages, at once hidden and open. Or an expression
on those features might run wild into the world, unmediated
by any mind, the reader's, who sat there in his cloak being
bothered by his fleas.

The word desired to be dulled. If not by the mind of this

or that reader, with or without fleas, then by the clapping shut of the book. Otherwise the pneuma might break out and be at large, tigerishly among the furrowed desks, or hopping mad in the muddy or sunbaked little village streets.

The book had covers to shield its pages from mud or sunlight. Not even fingers had any title to cross the track of the word. The covers also existed to contain the scorching majesty of the word. At least, a risk was set aside. Who knows, the majesty might otherwise choose to spill out as idiocy and make havoc, or too much heaven, among the huts.

It was also an offence to place one open book on top of another open book. The charms of the pneuma were inviolable, transcendental.

The light shoots shadows into this room, across the pages of books and a few squares of Philippino reed carpet. Somehow I love it so. Outside, the trunk of an elm spells out a green shadow across blades of grass, the quiverings of which can only be detected if you take the time to watch, if you truly care, if you quiver a bit yourself. The grass blades tilt at an inexplicable mass of angles. Their tips ought to be points, but actually are bitten off, because every so often I try to mow the shadows down and the mower's cruciform blade rips across them. Underneath the mower's metal casing the momentarily unseen, as grass, suffers this.

No matter. A sheet of paper on the desk surface carries the print of the insect screen, a tight cross-hatching. This keeps the little winged demons out and holds a whiteness in. Nothing written contradicts the self-sufficiency of the word; its complex force, noted only in various proximate oscillations, disdained by the flea, unapparent in action, otherwise in hope, is a fiction so threatening that we devise our most dazzling footwork to pull a little fruit out of the teeth of disaster.

Here, too, on this bitter grass near dusk I saw the cicada come into being. First it had made its long journey up a perpendicular tunnel to the earth surface; the cicada itself had lubricated the tunnel with a juice it exuded through its protective pupa. Now, inside the bronze pupa, which was crisping, a general shiver began to happen. An infinitesimal foot prodded a hole in the pupa, then another foot. Gradually the head was coming out, then the body, forwards, but for twenty minutes it made a lunge, rested, lunged again. Its moment of emergence was so prolonged that it could hardly be seen emerging. The motive and the power behind this effort – barely imaginable – I felt them in my groin as a sensation between craving and fright, then in my throat as a taste, brandy and pepper.

Finally, mute and dull, an oval pellet had shrugged the pupa off. The pellet put a leg out, soon another leg. Its back was turning emerald, then golden emerald, with wings that lay flush with the pellet, exceedingly frail, then larger, unfurling into twin networks of golden emerald filigree tracery. And the head, with eyes, had woken up, was turning this way and that way; now the wings could move and lift. The cicada glowed as if dusted with a pollen out of which, for the sake of argument, the breath of a beyond conjectured the world's first agile anatomies. Pristine forest contracted to the volume of a singing bird's egg. A fiery drop of universe at the other end of a tunnel through time.

So I lay down on the grass and put an ear to it. I was expecting the wings to rustle and give off a melodious twang, faint as the last echo of a Jew's harp in an Egyptian burial chamber.

Then it simply wasn't there. From high up in an elm its first ancient cackle fizzed into the onset of dark.

Svatava's Dream

Twice changed, forty years
Different country, different person

There I was, again, you must
Have heard me tell

How when I was eleven, all
The books of this old writer, how

Eagerly I read them, mystic, yet
Only now, back, beyond the river

Was I aware how close I was to him,
And found my way down cobbled

Lanes, twisting
Into his pink museum

Found some friends, a man, a woman
Had made a painting of a house

It was pink and breathing, walls
Went out and in, windows

Pink, the air was flowing out and
In again, I heard the sounds

The city sounds, just as ever
They had been, just as ever

But they said the house was mine
Mine if I wanted the pink museum

Yet the painting was my house
Here, not there, stone, this

House I live in, mine, of stone
It hurt me so to choose, I could not

Tell whose pink house was there or here
To be mine if I wanted

Was it for me, the old museum
The writer's mystical pink

And me eleven, was the picture
Where I am, or in a renovated

Hradshin room, was this a time
When you breathe fast and double

A time in the flush of being
A house you make with breath

Go pink and everything
For you are torn

The Turquoise

Somehow the memories fizzle out on us.
Large blank eyes of people starving.
A snatch of music soon
Will be Merida, the mirrored bedroom, not
The pang felt there, but a fountain
Touches palm trees. Pang –

I forgot how perception had to be
Wrenched from its
Regular socket: the speech of folds, eyewhite
And snow the robe a woman wore,
Foreign liquor
The smell of a man at noon in his hammock.

Raw stuff: a crooked
Line of objects. Look, it is put
Straight like hair by distance.
The whole shadow of (our tune) your smile
Oozed first from
Repetition on a jukebox. Careless

Memory cooks
The kind of meal you
Gulp down, because the right place
Had shut, or the old prices are
Out of sight. Compulsion
Turns you still

Back to the same town: the flies
In children's eyes are blue, the drowned
Horse prongs the air still,
Silver hoof; never sensing wrong,
The deadly salesmen frisk again
With girls in the disco.

Swat a fly, scratch the wall
Of an ear with a toothpick: four, suddenly,
The grouped figurines
Loom huge from the desk angle,
And glow, clay Chupicuaro, bronze
Krishna, the wooden African –

As gods. To construct them
Ancestors broke through their skins,
Getting this far at least: the rock
Crystal coyote, stud him
With turquoise, let the orange fire
Be a tail like a beacon;

For the unseen escapes,
The remembered
Dominion cracks, falsifies
Desire and presence as they fly screaming
Before us, headdress and tail
Bushy, slashing backward in the dark.

A Forge in Darkness

They hadn't forgotten his name
Or whereabouts the forge was,
The brick oven, hot glow
Of charcoal, the hammer floats
Up, held in mid-air now, and
What beer the old man drank.

A heart isn't like that. A heart
Won't wait until the dark
Comes to cool things off a bit.
It works through the blinding
Noon heat, careless of sparks,
Of hoofs clipclopping uphill.

Boys came by. Owls looked on.
A horse tail flicked at bluebottles,
Under the canopy of this pecan.
This hill – part of the night then,
A slope, that's all, crested with a forge,
Like a wave flecked with red foam.

What a letdown for her, hitched
To that limping, fretful man,
The reek of sweat and charcoal on him –
And her arms could take a whole sky in,
Her thumbs govern long ships or fondle lambs,
Yet she slid from her wave and under him.

It was here, right here, where I came
To be living. She's gone, he's gone.
I cook chicken where the forge
Must have been. In the dark I
Pour out more wine to remember
The little old lives of them.

Taking a chance, I think
That's where she must have gone:
Into the artifice of not forgetting
A name and what went on,
When the boys watched and owls
Heard the hammer come down.

6

Poems and Prose 1986-7

Michèle's Rooms

The handle of the willow basket curving
The red tiled unlevel trodden floor
At knee height the clock face but no clock body
Toy clock hands constant at twenty to six

The wooden bowl empty of apples
Balls and hanks of wool in the willow basket
The procession of sea urchin shells on the mantelpiece
The angled needles as they pierce the wool

In colored sleeves the shelved LPs
Loops of plants I came to water
Pink of the wool and of the towering candle
Snowy bear and rabbit warm for Lola

Rising suns of scallops knitted into a shawl
The way the shawl hangs unoccupied from a hook
A mobile by the window strung with wands and ducks
The tang of wine a moment held behind the teeth

The invisibility of the hook
The absence of electricity
The plant bowl that overflowed on the telephone bill
The tiny bird crouched on the mantelpiece

The lifted latch and the opening window
The breeze that burrows through a shirt for flesh
All these marks to detect her laughter by
The word's very event in a special voice

Curve of the beak of the sacred ibis
Heart of legend locked in a nondescript replica
Spheres that only come to thought as curves completely seen
Two cracks in the wooden beam darkening them

The wooden beam's edges bevelled by an old axe
Absent from the encyclopaedia the surge of the scribe's mind
Flit of the pen's tip crossing two scraps of paper
The ghostly scribe without a name

Another Almost

Almost it might be better
to forget the past than build
ruins out of ruins

Perhaps the ruins are forms
of a response too blocked or timid.
Who can figure a whole house?

Think of the first scavenging Turks,
incurious, they patched their huts
with odds and ends of temples

No, I mean it is tough going
always to remember
so little or too much

Then have it all, or some,
spring unbidden back into place.
The bundle of woe is heavy

Wave to me as I go,
inhabitants of memory,
from your ruins, houses, forests

Continue the story that broke,
somehow, in the middle.
Let me see, let me smell you

Intact to my hearing
perhaps you will open
zones of being I never knew

Mysterious flesh
might blossom, lost hills
tipped with frail churches

Mansions complete
with moats of liquid silver,
misty kitchens, whence

Incredible pastries issue, baked
in ovens I never saw,
wines I never drank

Might redden tables of real oak
in twilight courtyards –
all ordinary as now. So I bend

With an ache for you, child,
and one for you, my only love,
and another for Doyle, Irish pilot

Blown to bits on a rocket range.
More lovely or horrible
things I know

Happen to others,
I write this only to shorten
the time of a music

Which, unless I forget,
will mass ruin on ruin.
The watermill we slept in,

My other love, the rushing
water beneath us,
you had clipped my fingernails

So I forget it, forget, child,
the midnight we were frightened of.
I hoist on my back again

The bundle of woe, but first
I open it, a crack,
to see the bloody rags

And worn-out toothbrushes,
the splinters of bone
and a silver ring from Afghanistan

Which slid into a river;
I sniff the hair beside me,
I touch excited midnight skin

The time of a music
almost now I hear the spell of it
playing backwards

A Revenant

Now she is here
Again, quick, in a taste
Of lemon, not even so
Much as a bite, she is here
In a whiff

Of lemon peel, no way
Even to tell
Where from, the light
Saffron perhaps, a snowy
Touch of metal

Or, afloat
On a flood of being, me,
I had drawn
A tingle out, indistinct,
A distant signal

Flashing in the hotter rush
Of air tonight, mixed
Into it, funny,
Today, the wiggle
Of a child, head back

Shrimp bodysock, she
Did a glancing
Noonday
Dance across
A crack

In a paving stone, she
Shook
At the sky
Her fist
With a flower in it

Now so long dead
Another
Is here, I remember to be
In the taste
Or touch, or in the child

A wandering
Sensation, mutely
To learn my shape, later to flit
Ghostwise from a being
I will never know

Cybele

It is cold outside so she has walked in
Loving my feet for her own good reasons,

Straight in, tail up, scanning the kitchen
She discovers nothing but a desire

So at my feet she winds and unwinds
Her calico skin. When I tap on the blotter

Up she lifts a paw, forgets, listens again,
Looking elsewhere, if elsewhere is anywhere

And curls in a fit of abandon
Around the tongue of my tennis shoe.

Her paw milks the lace, her paw milks ankle bone,
Amorously unparticular she forgets her milk

Habit, suddenly crouches, licking her tail:
Suddenly I know nothing for her is sudden

For she forgets her forgotten tail, silent
She explores cavity, cavity, for instance

Behind the cutting block propped against
The wall, she has found a fascination

Shadow or moonlight there, scampers off
In a rage of vague desire for shadow

And foot, the raw smell of shadow and foot,
She's stepping over hollows everywhere

And finding what she wants to be hidden there,
Everything new, glistening cushion, clay

Horse, fragile, over it she has to step
A soft way. What invisible spasms of being

Span her heart beat? How come she detects
Here in this room the moon she only knows

From green by the shadows moon-eye makes
Nothing of? Smells are shape, the sharp

Outline of mouse, the cry of yucca white
She evidently smells when tasting my feet.

Not my feet. Them, me she ignores. It is
A very sweet crisis to be constantly cat:

Her senses, precise as Gieseking's fingers,
Track a music, her veins are shivering with it –

Transformation, the furnace of horror
Red in her claw, fact in her leap of fire –

She is arrow, target. The bird, a flit
She hesitates to hear, could prong her

Against a sky that is no sky for her
But promise of open, beak, edible, never

Depressive, it stings, strikes, white glistens.
Bone aches too that way in my meat.

An Ideologist

for David Edwards

Nebulous, fractured, not too fast,
How come this ring of hair
Falls to the white I doodle on.

If I turn it around by thought
I face unfeatured distance;
It hangs in the moon for luck.

Masts that were trees creak,
With cobalt sky bamboo combines,
And spiteful critics rule the roost:

Spirit is fierce, it contradicts,
Only a presuming, only a wizened
Spirit carps and backbites.

Attend. Soon my bamboo palace
Bathes in the pool that winked
From the fracture in that iron hair.

Unshod I see the earth, old nag,
Shake off its flies and epithets
And run like a cloud with the moon.

A Farewell in Old Mexico

Perhaps her husband was the engineer.
Palm up, timing perfect,
She waves to him. A hazel wave.
Here is the hand she cups, at the limit

Of an arm's curve, to catch his sooty kiss.
Animal black complex of intestines
Afloat on a thunderhead of steam, to the clank
Of twenty open trucks, you expelled

A hiss. Soon the sunflower field of faces
Lifts as one to swallow cool sierra air.
Wind sang star patterns into the grit.
On the boardwalk begonias inhabit tin cans;

Liquid, they are mirrored, even redder
In the sweat beading her top lip. The caboose
A dot, now she waves, with her comical
Sense of order, to it, not him.

The China Virgins

They tinkle in their glass
Voices more thin than shrill
Coils of mist they penetrate remote hill temples
They are fire tongues capping spires of thought
They inhabit oblongs of ice in orange juice

Often they appear when creation begins
In memory
They rub their fingers and glow when you lose your mule
Hungering footsore in a Tibet of aimlessness
Like an onset of birdsong in heartbreak they capture you

Cool outrush of force
In the construction of a seashell
Meandering prolonged across symmetry breaks
They delineate an evolution
They round the roof of a wren's nest

Pop of champagne cork
Snap of elastic against firm muscle
If not so then slow motioning the convolvulus display
Tremor of a voice when it has caught the drift
Of white bone powder blown across the Gobi

Breath of wind bending the crest of a catalpa
Also the clatter when catalpa bean pods fall
The sputter when wet has called for the surge
Of a body incandescent but then backs off
The china virgins recoil to advance

On the back of matter they pound their bright fists
Flash their eyes in the twice five parabolas of a Leticia's legs

A parchment swept by fingers
Sidereal coin
A nymph spinning struck into the hot silver centre
A song that drinks the scent of a space unborn
Nothing nothing but a phrase no sooner uttered
Than questioned as to its calligraphy
Nothing sooner questioned than the china virgins

The First Move

Looking through window glass at early light
Hearing The Moon Descend Over The Temple That Was
Combing space I feel a surge of hot day to come
A Mustang glides to the curb and stops
The driver rolls his window down and in my window's
Angle a shape so vague
Somehow it might have borrowed an absent limb
Is a man whose bent and only shadow spills across the tarmac

His tiny dog a solid sniffling at a bug I think
Still the Mustang driver through his other window
Parting foliage has to see the brick tower beyond

Has the clockwork stopped
Have they stopped their arguments and screams
Now what will the boiling corporals do
And the children too hungry to cry out

Flit of sparrow
Descending on seeds in the feeder east of me
Hand reaching out through the open Mustang window
A whole arm snaking out
The hand has touched the hot or cool car roof
The shadow on tarmac sharp as the dog's *Geruch*
Immobile as this bergamot in a smoky taste of tea
Me immobile feeling through window glass
How absently till now I have clawed at life

Unchanged the light identical the suspense
Whoever moves first will make the first move

The Image

When they finally got around to where they had begun, it
wasn't there any more. This was because they'd strung it
out behind them. What had been a chariot of fire had
become a rickety old wagon. Losing its parts as it bumped
along, wheels breaking, then dropping off, the rest of it a
carcass of broken axles, bleached boards, rusted prongs
and rotted leather cinches, it had eventually, without anyone noticing when it happened, disconnected itself, then
vanished into thin air. It would have made not a scrap of
difference if someone had been delegated to keep an eye
on it, down the years. They never should have hitched it
up, to be hauled behind them, in the first place. So now
they looked around, checking the latitude. Forgetfully they
wondered where it might have gone. Might they have mis-
calculated their position? Had they drifted or been driven

262

off course? There had been hazards, they could have been driven off course; they could have drifted, there had been spates of negligence. But no, they had arrived at the exact same spot, this was where they'd begun. There were no signs of the four rivers, no views of the mountain. As for the temperate climate some of the old hands had spoken of, now there came over them a blizzard, biting cold, now the withering oven heat of the desert.

La Morena

My white cow tonight is quite silent
My white cow milking a heart from darkness

What tricks and silks will she tumble into
My white cow with opening parachute lips

My white cow with a shirt of woodsmoke
My white cow with a beehive of desires

Sometimes an abandon seizes her by the horns
Sometimes she is placid and sings in church

My white cow dancing in her field of fire
My white cow walking with dangerous steps

Everywhere she supposes there are cathedrals
Everywhere bells inscribe on air their spiral signs

My white cow with marked ideas of her own
My white cow whose tuft is a tangle of tempers

The baskets of air hang from her solid bones
The jugs of earth lift with her little breasts

My white cow who makes sorrow burn a day away
My white cow who makes sorrow bite like a shark

My white cow who shivers and penetrates men
My white cow who rides men bareback

Often conscious of too many things at one time
Often come times when she knows nothing at all

She has no clock for her timing is internal
No voice but hers alone tells her when and how

She will eat dry bread if there's none better
My white cow who tastes always of oranges

My white cow who goes one better than the snow
Her quim is heaven for whom she pleases

In the nights we stretch with furious argument
My white cow takes every word to its limit

Shortening days we walk together hand in hand
More than once she tore my arm from its socket

I will do my dance one-armed for my white cow
I love her life her ways her difficult nature

We live beneath roofs that stand centuries apart
My white cow in small towns and purple cities

My white cow in a village dances to the guitar
My white cow sipping wine from a cup of clay

When the baskets are hanging bright in the water
They fill with her fish and creak in earthquake

When in my white cow's hair old stories are told
We stop them to start the world afresh redeemed

She is absent in the canyon of her red lust
She is present in the ordinary dishes we eat off

My white cow is a black one to tell the truth
Or else Chinese or else some kind of Arabian

To call her a cow at all is a profound mistake
She is a leopard with four cubs in a forest

My white cow in that hotel stripping off her clothes
My white cow who is not mine at all

My white vanishing cow with her dolphin legs
My white cow who wades *toute nue* in the Toulourenc

Her skin mirrors itself and that is it for us
I fall into her skin to oblige Lord Shock

I tongue my white cow in her purity and playfulness
She will never come around to believing I mean it

My white cow imagines me far off running away
Little does she know I run to catch her leaping form

White cow who dances wild in the middle of the world
White cow your sweet dust with the wind blowing over it

From Earth Myriad Robed

1

Why do I hide from this? I see two sides of what I hide
from. On one side a sheet of flame. On the other side a
violet horn or the horn of a violet (sharper ears might figure
which) would have to envelop no secret oil, no quintessence,
but a leg of lamb. Then the obstacle flies apart. Out of this
horn a pit is made, and the pit exhales a sizzle and three
puffs of smoke. But in Madrid a great lady sits, back straight,
on her terracotta throne, and she is on both sides. From
her, too, I have been hidden. I was hidden from her slow
phantom pace through her costumes in history, from the
shock of her arrival – from the contraction of her excavated
splendour into the clay, this instant. What hid will not be
me if only I can touch, without breaking it, a single contour
of the uncontainable.

Most probably the cook had built it with forethought. The scheme haunting his mind might have been Praxitelean, but he fattened that scheme with fierce Turkish caprice. The skeleton sparkled in the depths of his daydreams and a two-pronged plot, just as probably, rose to the forefront of the cook's mind when he balanced his resources against the fortune he might pocket, once his caprice could be made flesh, fully apparent.

The indoors aspect of his restaurant bore on its lintel an inscription in bold Latin capitals: TURKISH KITCHEN DELICATES FİŞİS AND KEBAP. Outside there was dusty space enough for a flock of goats. Here he shook sackfuls of cement into a revolving iron egg. Here he hosed water into the egg for to make a heavy cement paste. With a shovel he turned the cement until it was hardening. Then did he create with it a circular pond to contain water deep enough for fişis therein to outlive the blaze of day. Therefore into the centre of the pond he plunged a pump to circulate the water and to cool it as it flowed. Now he constructed a raised channel with more cement. In the form of a square he constructed it, to frame the dusty space, his kitchen, water chuckling as it flowed anticlockwise along the channel contained by the low walls he clapped into shape with a board. Not otherwise had aforetimes lavish Aegean air circled columns in the peristyle of a temple, to cool the violet interior, where dwelled, ever fresh, in his happiness, at his repose, the god.

Then came the long branches of eucalyptus trees, for the cook did send forth a throng of boys to gather branches from the shore, weathered branches, none thicker than a boy's wrist. And they did gather many; that throng of boys barefoot gathered many and laid them for him in the dust. Now did he trim the branches and he did prop them one against another and he did fix the uppermost twigs and lock them together like the antlers of Hittite stags, and he spaliered the branches on a tilt to support, across a sloped continuous ridge, two long strips of plastic guttering, one above the other, the lower strip concave, the upper strip flat, as a shelf for flasks of orange and lemon juice. Between these gutterings, just above a man's height, he lodged eight empty plastic bottles on their sides, not all of one same capacity, no, but none less than a gallon bottle. He did then perforate each bottle, top and base, so that, once he had coupled the bottles, water soon would flow from one into the next, the first or eighth being the largest and blue, the others being without colour save for their red screw tops. Experimentally then did he let water into the blue bottle and it flowed, through the other seven, at various velocities, none too fast, finally to gush from a spout, made of a shining shoe horn, back into the circular fishpond. Now did he verily set the pump to work and with a great splutter the circuit sprang to life. Water pumped from the pond flowed along the framing channel of low walls and rose by its own motion and pressure into the blue bottle, chugged through the other seven bottles, and dropped back down the shining shoe horn spout into the pond again.

There was also a shade tree set not far back from the blue bottle. To the stout trunk of this tree he did now fasten with clamps of lustrous tin a vertical neon tube, for the shedding of light upon the scene, when twilight should have descended. And he tucked an insulated flex, black and thick, between the tree trunk and the neon tube; all the way back to the roof of the restaurant he then did run the flex in a loop. Out of the flex he teased the wires of fine copper and from these he did hang half a dozen fairy lights, red, yellow, and blue, for now too the electricity could flow, not, he hoped, intermittently, as is its habit thereabouts, but steadily, so that with a certain aurora the fairy lights would sponge the smoke and dust of his arena.

Hard by his cooking pit in the dust he did hang a bell from a spike, and to this bell he tied a cord, the other end of which he fastened somewhere else, so that from almost anywhere in his arena he could pluck the cord and ring the bell. Across the dust, his centre of command, next he did trundle a big tin box with a turning spit in it, and afterward he set beside it with a loud clink, like that of an armoured man bounding into the saddle, an icebox containing a squadron of tincapped beverage bottles. Swigging vigorously from one of these he swung his arms, lifted and stamped his feet, thus and thus; so did he school his waiters not to trip but to skip or pirouette across the walled water channel at his bell's behest. As in a bastion there he now stood, plucking on his cord. Like acrobats the waiters bore aloft to his guests their flashing trays of food and drink, and his guests were ravished to be served nocturnally by such nimble acrobats.

Then did he put on his hat, not stiff and tall like the hat of an hotel cook, but flat and floppy, almost like the hat of a sailor. He took in one hand his long knife and with one stroke severed clean in half a lamb's backside; and anon with his long fierce fork he pronged into my mouth a lamb's testicle, hot from his grill, a gift. He waved his net into the fishpond and pulled a fat fish out, the length of a cubit, a sea trout, and the fish writhed in the net. Its glittering flesh was firm and cold to my touch, and all the while woodsmoke poured from his pit into my nostrils I could taste times out of mind; I saw a web of wrinkles run across the gong-smooth face of a nomad girl and turning into a tiny globe the solo hoot of an Andalusian owl; in a bellshaped, windshook, goatskin tent I lay and heard breath quicken, faster and faster the thump of coupling.

In the second or seventh plastic bottle the cook had housed a young turtle. Gazing far into the night, measuring his mighty words, he did prophesy that when the turtle was grown so big, so big, then would it burst its bottle, then would come the moment, the countertrigonometrical moment, at which every particle he had raised into manifestation would in a flash attain perfection and so melt away, retrieved by the infinite. For then, too, the insulation of the fairy light flex, burned through by the neon's gentle heat, would perish, the shade tree would explode in a sheet of flame and everybody would be electrocuted. Yet for that moment the blaze would everywhere transfigure the night, even far out at sea, so nobody would mind: the glory of the world when it ended would have no end, and if people grieved at all, they would grieve only during that one moment, haply on account of the turtle being boiled to a turn with nobody there to eat it.

3

Rope sole of a razouteur. Dust beaten out of it. A puff of
dust beaten out of a rope sole in a small French hotel, old
oak beams overhead. In the puff of dust, vestiges of a village
dancing floor. A dancing floor in the dust in a land soaked
in blood. The features of Elif: mop of tight black curls, dolphin eyebrows, immense dark eyes, small straight nose,
her breath from lips parting. Elif in her satin dress, pale
gold satin with a blue sash. And the pounding of the music,
in the village dust, the puff of dust gone, Elif gone, into
the smoke.

The moment of the pigeon when it hovers in the white
zenith of a fountain, splashed, uncontainable, the moment
of the pigeon. The moment of the wave when it crests. The
moment when the wave peaks, mountainous, and orches-
trates its prisms to catch the flying light.

The straight back of Elif dancing, all ten years of her,
the milling motion of her hands, prints of her bare feet in
the dust. A full moon had risen, its globe slowly flew over
the distant headland. Smoke from the fire, woodsmoke.
The moment of the fat when it spills into embers and the
smoke went up, a white flock of smoke, when the smoke
is wool, when the owl hoots, when Elif is a lamb, when
she mills her hands, as if winding wool with fingers of
spindle, wrists arched like ibis beaks.

The throne she sat in was of wood and canvas. She sat
in it on the far side of the fire, chin in hand. At a sign she
flew across dust between the young men dancing and back
again holding in each hand an empty beer bottle. Prints of
her bare feet in the dust, erased by the stamping of feet in
razouteurs. The throne she sat in was terracotta or maybe
stone. She sat with her back straight, wearing a pale gold
satin dress, for tonight, the moment when it was tonight,
she had not remembered to wear her Ishtar headscarf. And
as she flew again across the dust of the dancing floor, she
held in each hand a foaming beer bottle.

I had not made any sign to her, but now she stood near.

She spoke, at first with a little smile, in surges, at times in leafy whispers, now and then with cries, low but sharp, apparently in a gibberish she was inventing, but always as if it was a great adventure to speak. Some phrases I heard as Greek, others as Turkish. Several sounds I must have misheard, glossing them as English, but her voice drew them up, I thought, while she sang them out, from an origin as indistinct as Hurrian. As she spoke she pointed a finger, this way and that.

     – Tais da efendim (so she said, standing near)
       bu ghejeh
       ti theleis ti theleis efendim
       surleyebilir musunuz yakoondala

     – oosa ana tanta asnula kyriye
       ishmek ishki inghiliz tek ort poro
       tek ort poro yabanchuh . . . ti theleis?

     – aire kai philia
       aire kai kypris
       kuruk chok su
       kuruk adam efendim

     – Poompanul
       poompan simi not

     – him father fall down rock
       sky him all hurt
       nunca nunca

     – ek te homileo
       ek te midolor homileo
       lütfen bu yazar
       midolor yazar midolor insan dolor

     – nehden nehden selene
       io nata ikon elithosiniu
       sema athanato sema polychrono
       io nata io nata chabuk oosa
       ana kai roon . . . ula roon . . . kai karanlik
       yok palas . . . tek lokanta poro

Here she ran off across a corner of the dancing floor, vanished into an invisible room behind the canvas throne, and soon she was coming back through the smoke with a bowl of ice and another bottle of rakı. She set them silently on the table and for moments she stood and looked, tilting her head, and did not speak, did not move. Then with three fingers forming a little trefoil-like triangle, once and lightly she struck the silver Berber talisman on my chest, and she was whispering again:

> – baba
> baba ti linos mi linos . . . halk müzik
> tok asnula singtok
> singit rhythmon dalul danstokala
> tok thether baba . . . ti linos . . . benim müziyim
> thayat awa billes singis binot killet
> binot killet . . .
> ne akshamleyin ne de sabahleyin

And then her lips closed and she was gazing at the sky. Her throat moved as if she were swallowing, and when she looked at me again she was saying

> – dans kuklon
> kuklon dans
>
> – lütfen bu yazar . . . bu yazar
>
> – sikilos efter poh . . . seeyin
> ahas longas yulif . . . shine
>
> – shimdi gitmem lazum

And she did have to go, her father called to her; huge faces lit by candle flames change their shapes, people feasting sit at long tables in a semicircle, and she is running among them, carrying plates of lamb and fish and cabrito, keeping the glasses full.

Stamping of the feet and stretching the arms out, hand on a hip and hand in the air, the click of the fingers has to perpetuate something, a form, a throb from the footsoles touching the dust and rushing a wave up through the midriff into the shoulders, darkening the blood contained by the domes of the fingertips clicking brushed by the ball of the thumb where from the centre printed in skin tissue the spiral branches out, flesh to its limit carries the pulse and the dance measure remembers a labyrinth, even though we dance rough, whooping and hooting, the land is soaked in blood, the circle is broken and we stumble only fractions of it...So that was why these peoples dance in a circle, even two by two inviting memory of a circle – otherwise they might totter singly away, stringing out, lost forever in the distances of Asia, as others are lost in individuality. And there was a tomb far off, brooding vacantly; more near, undiscovered, a seashell had evolved from its node. A bud of rose, a tomb's peaked lid, I remember these, for now the moment of the pigeon makes the twin peaks of Elif's upper lip more than those alone. More now than purely thoughtful she came back, just once, she came back and chose to give me her hands. I would have heaped them with apples, but none grow there. I would have given her a flock of silky black tinkling goats, a box of stories and sketchbooks and pencils, rolls of embroidery, bushels of wheat, her school fees, an orchard I would have given her, a family of ponies in it, but, as it is, I take her suffering with me, and stupidly I tell her "Ya no hay remedio," for a wind in reverse, enormous cyclone, pulls her backwards into the future, pretty soon its teeth will have torn her wings off. Hearing behind her the howl of that wind, Elif has become an outline against a rose trellis, a figure unwinking, mantled, enthroned, in a faraway tomb frieze, and now I'm gone, the dust is nowhere, Elif nowhere, stretching her arms out. The dust, with her long gaze she has fathomed it.

4

The shadow of abstraction lifts from the writing. It is joined soon by the shadow of emotion. The shadows mix, penetrate one another, and obliterate everything, everything except the sound of writing. This is not the clatter of keys, not the yawns of the mouth mouthing words that call to be written. She had told me, Elif had told me, *bu yazar*, write this down.

You don't yawn in the face of an Elif: she had said her sorrow is the people's sorrow, *insan dolor*.

As the shadows lift and mix, another phrase is obliterated: *tek ort poro*. I hear it again and am being told – This place is a limit, a threshold. To the sound of writing I must reduce that limit. The sound is not the scratching of a head, not the creak of a chair, not knees cracking. A dust devil spins over an oblong of flowers which wait to be named. Never heard a dust devil sound like that before. A dust devil spinning over bushy oblongs of flowers waiting to be named.

So the male imagines that he constructs, but finally a negative will, till then secret, pops out. Protective the female stands in the circle of dust, juggling oranges; she cups a hand and fields with it the fierce male shots, to add one orange after another to her circus of oranges. Has Ahab heard the scream of Queequeg dying? Ahab has heard the scream and peglegs below deck to discover, tattooed over Queequeg's body, the map of a whole tribal universe. Suddenly Ahab has discovered this universe in the scream too. He brandishes his whalebone cane, shakes his repaired leg, orders his ship about, the China Seas are soon behind, the distances disappear, and instead of a whale it is oranges for Ahab. He has arrived in Valencia, he will spend the September of his life juggling oranges, more and more of them, standing in a dusty square. While Queequeg, recovered, tosses oranges to Ahab, Ahab juggles them, to re-enact for pleasure the whole tattoo inscribed in Queequeg's skin. It is the sound of writing. The sound of writing is the whizz of the oranges, the swish of flails beating flax, it is the thud of feet which dance for the life of Linos, so she said, so Elif said, on the threshold, and for the bondage of Linos to death, of which she said nothing. So we speak of linen and bond. So we do scratch the air until, out of it, come the shouts of the Great Shining Cook of Dalyan, in response, giving no mercy, to the whisper of a spirit in Patara.

273

Le Déjeuner

A description of a painting...has to begin. With an assertion.
If, to see this big square painting, you stand on your head
– in the Jeu de Paume it used to be permitted – you may
see features not otherwise seen. From the top descends a
hemisphere of shadow; from the bottom ascends a hemisphere of light. The shadow permeates sparse tree foliage,
a French window-door with shutters pinned back to the
wall on each side of it, a summer hat apparently hung in
a closer tree, a border of geraniums, and a flowering shrub
in a footed green box. The light permeates a table, over
which a cloth of white linen has been spread, a fruit bowl
with a tall stem standing on the table, then a blue coffee
cup, it permeates a wine glass, off-centre a silver coffee pot
with a looped handle (little echo of the hemisphere, set on
a black tray), elsewhere another coffee cup, then a large
white rose and a small one on the hither side of the table,
at which a trolley stands, a trolley with a basket top, the
basket top containing a shallow bowl of fruit, a wine glass,
and a brioche from which a slice has been cut.

Shadow dapples the table cloth. The fruit bowl with
the tall stem breaks the curve of the table and so is sharply
outlined in the middle ground left of centre against the soft
orange of the sunlit garden path. Shadow in the upper part
of the painting is also lightened toward the right by the
white hanging hat and a white exploding rose held against
the hat crown by the long black hat ribbon.

The effect of the hemispheres is only marked if you
stand on your head. If you do not stand on your head, you
will probably see only, or glimpse – boundaries here are so
moulded as to suggest, by restraining it, a pressure from
the abundance secreted by things, which, if it broke free,
would bury everything in a dazzling avalanche of aura – a
diagonal from top left to bottom right separating shadowy
from sunlit areas, for it passes across the orange path to
bury itself in the folds of a white parasol which has been
deposited on the seat of a curved and slatted garden bench.
A complementary diagonal, and a more quivering one, passes
from the bottom left corner, through the tiny easel to which

a little squatting boy attends, beneath the table and across a clump of flowers; beyond the flowers it finds two women, between the women a forked green space echoes the dark forked folds of the parasol. This diagonal loses itself in the stomach of the woman robed in yellow, then it reappears, to arrow the short remaining distance up through more foliage and strike the top right corner of the painting.

Happily the crossing diagonals are not so marked as to hint of deletion. Yet there was to have been a lunch and now the brioche is barely nibbled on, there is wine reddening the bottoms of both glasses, the cups are not darkened by coffee. Did the heavy yellow woman interrupt the lunch? Did the slender woman in white, now wearing a formal, turret-shaped and forward-tilting hat, run to meet her and remember while she ran that, Oh, a guest had been invited? Had the slender white woman, now so formal, only minutes ago flung her hat with rapture into the branches – before the heavy visitor rapped twice on an invisible door with an inaudible brass knocker?

There can have been no lunch to speak of, only some commotion.

Suddenly the painter saw the picture, flung his copious linen napkin on the table, shoved his chair back across secret orange gravel he's now standing on, fished his brushes out and began to paint. It was he, too, who disrupted lunch. Now he dissolves into its components the instant of commotion which instigated his insight. He has caught the flying instant as an aura contained in coloured objects, transfixed by two diagonals, and cushioned by two polarizing hemispheres. The picture presents the permanent dance of particles inside the shell of a disruptive incident. No time for lunch.

Two women, two cups, two wine glasses, two roses, a handbag on the bench beneighbours the parasol, the hat ribbon trails two extremities. And the little boy squats on the ground, contentedly alone at his tiny easel; his partner is papa, the painter, a pair of hands at an invisible easel in the most impenetrable fold. The painter, transparent. You

275

see not him but his insight. Sitting or standing, he will have been where you have come to be. A descant.

Another descant: from the depths of a dark Algerian mosque two voices alternating, one broken, old, but gradually swelling, the other, young, streaming from above, Isabelle Eberhardt heard them flash in her as they combined to complete a circuit which discharged in her 'almost an ecstasy'.

The heavy woman was a disruptor too. The painter deals with her. He paints her as an immobile vast chrysalis of a faintly golden hue. She is no mere marginal part of the web of the picture. The spider painter caught her in his web, his *toile d'araignée*. Also the hat, the incongruous hat hung in the tree, he catches it so deftly that, if you block it out with a hand, the web, for all its shimmering tonal affinities, lacks flourish, has been drained of elasticity.

So the hat was flung up there for joy, not by the lady before the forgone lunch began, not by her, but by the painter, who picked up, from the ground where Delacroix had tossed it, Jacob's hat, picked it up and flung or floated it into the glory of his web, and while sailing upward it was transformed from a well-worn Hebrew shepherd hat, curly-brimmed, heavy with dust and sweat, to become a debonair Val d'Oise summer hat in 1874, from whose crown cascades a wide ribbon, black, but since its ends are fluttering, divided, this black isn't death, it is trousers, with sinuous legs in them, describing the double-step of a dance. Jacob's angel has been retired – blushing – into the chrysalis with a faintly golden hue.

The story can't be told otherwise than by a seclusion. The disruption of the normal incident, a lunch, can't be accounted for, until in his memory the painter reconstitutes the disruption and imagines, with marks that play across the web from all sensitive angles, seldom in sequence, the impact of an intensity that only came to be lifesize when he saw there was something doubly abundant he'd forgotten.

7

From *The Pursuit of the Kingfisher* (1983)

LOUISE MOILLON'S APRICOTS (1635)

She has allowed the absolute standpoint of a twenty-year-old woman to be consumed by a heap of apricots in a long basket. The apricots in their basket are on a table, the front edge of which is paler than its remoter edge; and here on the front edge there are drops of water, five of them, at one of which a fly is sipping. The spectacularly detailed little fly is wearing wings of a delicately veined fabric.

The other drops of water, various in size, are in that perfect condition which precedes eruption or evaporation. They, in their way, though transparent, are as radiantly corporeal as the apricots.

To the left of the group of four drops of water there is an apricot that has been sliced open; the kernel is still attached to its hollow in the one half. To the right of the fly's drop, there are two apricots, whole, and across them a leafed twig is placed, while attached to the flyward end of the twig are two dark purple shining fruits, probably plums.

Every visible apricot has a bloom, but only on a few is this bloom so noticeable as to be almost an aura. The basket which contains the apricots is made of dark, aged reeds. The apricots stand, or rather they configure, against a background which is black, opaque, impenetrable. Is it really a heap of apricots? Their golden and rotund volumes are casually consorted; it is not so much a heap as an ordering of apricots. Some are resting, each one at its own tilt or angle, on others which are lodged in the middle of the heap, and still others can be seen as a third and remoter group, closer to the darkness. The tripling of the picture space, darkness upward and behind, golden rounds in the middle, and in the foreground the pale brown table surface and edge, is apparent also in this terracing of the apricots.

It is thinkable that she ordered the apricots in this fluid recessive way, each apricot with its twin rondures meeting in the tender sweep of its crease, even though not many display this crease, so as to discourage any donjuanesque

279

counting of the apricots; but also in anticipation that someone, sooner or later, would be certain to count them, someone would ascertain that there are twenty-nine apricots in the basket, and that the number twenty-nine is one of those that are not divisible without a rupture of number into fractions.

There are, however, eight apricots that are so placed as to show the crease, nine, if the apricot on the far right, outside the basket, and on the surface of the table, is included. Also the apricot farthest to the left, but only second highest in the heap, diagonally across from the other, has a crease that is set at a contrastive angle to that of the lower right-hand apricot. The two halves of a circumflex accent, drawn apart, anchor thus each extremity of the left-to-right diagonal from heap to table. It is thinkable that she put her own cocked eyebrow, interrogatively, into the picture.

What is more, the fluid recessive triple-terraced heap of twenty-nine apricots rests in a lining, or nest, of leaves. This nest is hardly noticed at first. Each leaf has sharp, staggered points, six or more. The group of leaves across the top of the heap is not so fresh; no crisp points. These leaves, against the opaque dark background, look wilted, they are contaminated, perhaps by the darkness: one of them is only half a leaf, the absent half has been eaten away, and another has a distinct black hole in it.

Apart from a subjection of certain leaves to an alien and tainting mouth, what can be felt? The spikiness of the leaves around the apricots warns any mouth that all is not so sweet and velvety as one might suppose; as one might suppose, on seeing with one's mouth, even before the eyes have come to the matter, that the seductively edible, creased and golden fruits are for all the world like virgin quims, waiting to enjoy and to be enjoyed. She is saying: Don't you be so sure, these curves are analogues of us, curved ribs, which even our creator could or would not lean upon to make straight. But as a woman she was saying also to women: In you, bodies, there is the presence, a treasure; too soon a leaf goes limp, too late the spikes bristle against the intrusive prick, the eyeballs –

Because the subject is so familiar, you might hang this picture in your kitchen for a year or two and never notice, never really care. The one care might be for the drops of water and the fly. She spent more time lavishing her skill and attention on them, than could ever have been encompassed by any actual co-existence of theirs on the forward edge of the table. Here, too, the accent of her eyebrow, putting a question. Or the diagram of a prolonged insight, a frenzy transfixing an instant, makes the presence violently manifest, as wonder. No, that cannot be it, that cannot be exactly it. A noun phrase or two cannot reflexively represent what she perceived and created as a complex hypotactical sentence, dominated by an as yet uninvented verb-series.

Green and gold, spiked leaf and vulnerable *mons*, the tainting dark and the dance of apricots across the kitchen, forgotten, explored, what happened, Louise, you were a Protestant, in the Cevennes I have seen the museum of the desert where the atrocities inflicted upon your people are commemorated. Actually your eyebrows circumflexed a mystery which we have still not chattered away: Is the presence real, do intervening mediations obliterate it, have we not yet invented any language for it? Is nothing immediate? When it happens, now, and someone coming into the kitchen suddenly winces at the shock of a new cell originating in his brain, that sharp shock, is it paintless and nameless? Or is it graduable into ontological regions, subtle removes, the provinces of difference?

Bless you, do not see wounds as apricots inflicted on the darkness, no, I meant to put it the other way. Place yourself otherwise; be vigilant, but without anxiety, which means – do not interfere with it, let your folds unfold to envelop that force, though it is terrible, mind your reed basket is ventilated and does not dry out. The basket exists for the ordering of apricots, it is the cage of ribs in which each one of them contends for its time, the apricots, which are not weightless, they press against one another, and only the drops of water, really, fly up, evaporating. The fly, the fly is a heavy being, a twinge in the bruise. Of that bruise the two plums are telling, also otherwise, soothed by the twig that is laid horizontally across them, a touch. But look: where the twig was torn off, a flitch of white shows, another wound, the lowest factor, in the right-hand corner, a curl of white, or a snarl, ridiculously completing all the curves of all the apricots.

Again, begin to read the apricots. Because the deeper tones of gold are among those on the right, and these tones are in an ironic concord with the darkness of the ground, you will respond to a compulsion to reverse the mechanics of any European text – and see from right to left. The creases in the apricots obligingly shift their angles that way also, relatively clockwise. Yet, having made this reversal, you wonder why you made it, why you did not read from the relatively stronger illumination of the apricots on the left, why you did not swivel your eyes then slowly to the right, following an anti-clockwise jerking of the creases toward the deeper tones, unbinding the spell of time.

Precisely that act of wonder suspends any absolute viewpoint – with nothing lost to indeterminacy. This is the threshold across which Keats listened to the nightingale, and on which he constructed, for wonder, a Grecian urn, which also had three groups of figures, deities, or mortals, or both, in frozen ecstasy around it. Louise put her fly on that threshold, in relation to the absolutes of levity – the tight-skinned drops of water; and to the collapsible, heavy, fugitive fly corresponds, in other mythologies, the prince of all metamorphosis, the frog.

Her liminal fly, her to-be-absolute water-drops, her present apricots, and this great bruising darkness – all the visible, little, fugitive bodies enact in a configuration the magic of an oneiric etymology. 'Abri' – shelter, dark shield, death a refuge, at least, and 'cot' – a more miniscule non-lexical non-seme could hardly exist. There could be no lighter consonant, no rounder vowel, than in the sound of 'co[t]'. It has no gravity of signification at all. Yet that non-word's oneiric axis generates a small whirl of shadowy relatives: Rabelaisians might find that it verges toward a word now lost, 'cotal', meaning penis; 'coter' is what surveyors and engineers have to do, measuring land for buildings, plotting a site for a construction; and 'cotir' – sometimes for rustics, even if this one did not know it until this very instant when he looked it up – means 'to bruise', as a fruit is bruised.

REFLECTIONS ON A VIKING PROW

1

To recapture poetic reality in a tottering world, we may have to revise, once more, the idea of a poem as an expression of the 'contents' of a subjectivity. Some poems, at least, and some types of poetic language, constitute structures of a singularly radiant kind, where 'self-expression' has undergone a profound change of function. We experience these structures, if not as revelations of being, then as apertures upon being. We experience them as we experience nothing else.

Yet we say that a poetic text is not this or that thing out there. We say that such a virtual thing as a text is not an actual thing, that it is not even thinglike at all. Or we say that this or that text occupies an interface between things and persons, but has its ontological status only c/o the addressee, who is itinerant and anonymous. Look at the problem this way: Might it be that we are forgetting what a thing as artifact firstly is and secondly signifies? We might be forgetting, in particular, about the intrinsic virtues of pre-industrial artifacts, not only ones that had explicitly sacred value.

Lace, icons, handblown glass, handstruck Greek coins, bone implements, masks, figurines, old books, paintings, carts, and bedspreads and ploughs – such handmade things are real, did become real, because they were brought to life by currents of formalized energy, desire crystallizing as it passed from imagination to skilled hands, through to treasured materials, and back again in a circuit never broken. Some artifacts were charged with a 'spirit' which, as in Kwakiutl masks, formalized itself while the skill of the artificer conducted it, like lightning, and crystallized it into socially significant objects illuminating the whole time/space context of the artificer and his tribe. Such an artificer is not confessing, not foregrounding his own subjective

283

compulsions, not cataloguing impressions, not hanging an edict from an anecdote. There is nothing random which is not absorbed into the structure of the artifact. The artificer fashions a group wisdom in the thing which speaks for itself.

That is, at least, one way of viewing, now, certain objects and practices older than ours and other than ours. We may dismiss such practices as fetishism. Seldom do we recognize the watery fetishism, or idolatry, that we ourselves bring to bear on cars, washing-machines, cigarette lighters, a glittering host of technoid commodities. The older practices were informed by vigorous, even fierce animistic feeling about the materials at hand, the wood, the jade, the bronze, to which people could relate as once to animals and to the gods in animals. The animism may not always have been lucid. At least it resourcefully furnished knowledge through the conduit of the material, as we can still see in old cathedrals. Our practices are evidently less animate. We fetishize commodities on the basis of yawning indifference – or tight-lipped hostility – toward a world of objects that confuse perception and multiply signs of our alienation. Yet, worse, faced with this forbidding world, bothered by it, we finally cease to care. The profit motive, blunted by high taxation, sees to it that we seldom take joy in putting body and soul into things we make for sale or even for our own consumption. A tiny fraction of the mass world, west or east, can still find gratification in handmaking perfect things in leisure time stolen from money time. Artisanal work is coming back, yes, and in the USA, of all places, a little good cooking. But the mainline production mechanisms keep these changes peripheral, for an élite. For the rest: plastics and apathy, sinister twins. Plastix and Apathy: twin *croque-morts* stuffing the corpse of Western civilization.

The old animistic practices, the old view of *things*, had a great range of vital significance: from witchcraft to Rilke, from soothsaying to apparel, from Viking ships to the most delicate French and German portrait miniatures of the later eighteenth century. The artifact as icon: if you lived in that world, an icon actually contained for you the soul-substance of the person portrayed. Portrayal was not descriptive or derived. It was presentation, immediate and precise, of the being resonantly invoked by the image and stored in the image. There was more to this than idolatry. By the image the viewer was freed from some snags in the circuitry of response to the world, snags which for us stop growth in two general ways. One is the opacity, compounded of dread and habit, which bottles subjectivity up. The other is the NOHOW feeling which liquefies subjectivity. No wonder that throughout the 1840s hundreds of thousands of North American people rushed into the daguerreotype studios, hoping to achieve structure, identity, in the form of a perfect and detailed image.

I must edge away from this frame of reference to approach another question. It may be impossible to reconstruct exactly an older world's quasi-magical reality, the texture of its beliefs. But we can do so conjecturally, in this case, by asking how artifacts behaved, or else were thought to reach out and touch the boundaries of space, physical and social space, which defined them. First I shall outline a conjecture, then trace correspondences between that touch relation (artifact/environment) and poems experienced as apertures upon specific spaces, or places.

Artifact and environment: a dramatic example is the prow of the Oseberg Viking Ship. The photo I'm looking at as I write shows a curved piece of wood, elaborately carved, sweeping up out of the rocks and mud which buried the ship for eleven centuries. Placed in receding layers behind the carved wooden curve, secured by the wooden plugs, are eight boards, quite slender, the front of the hull, their own curve following the axe-edge upward curve of the prow. Then comes another carved board, as if to reinforce the significance of the prow board. The leading edge of the prow board is about as wide as a kitchen matchbox. It is blank and is paralleled by another blank, the trailing edge. Inside this frame come the carved figures.

The figures are carved in low relief, curlings and weavings and interlacing, dragonlike designs. On what is left of the prow board you can count seven major areas, interlocking. The anterior reinforcing board, eight boards back, has a similar but not identical configuration of interlaced and interlocking squirls, tendrils, sticklike ligaments, and broader body-areas – again dragonlike. This figuration is not representational. It is something else, but what? The body-areas are cross-hatched all over, with striations less deep than the squirl outlines: little elevated rectangles, like those which are concave ('coffered') in a waffle – dragon scales, if dragons were intended at all. But nowhere does this intricate ornamentation obliterate the woody nature of the wood. You can see the grain. Nowhere, either, does the carving weaken the wood. You see what they mean, the etymologists who derive from the word 'cosmos' the word 'cosmetic'. Essential virtù explicit in accented palpable form.

People say that the dragons, whose claws invariably point outward to the sea, were meant to protect the oarsmen from evil spirits. I would go further. The dragons are sea foam formalized into (mythic) animal shapes. They are animal formalizations of the sea foam that crashes against the prow or lies briefly on the ocean surface. At the same time, the dragons in no way deform the wood. They are realized directly out of the wood and its grain. The carver carved the protoforms of sea substance into the wood, because then, he thought, even if portrayed as dragons, these protoforms, at home in the wood, know also how to deal with the sea, they being made of the sea, while sharing too the life of the wood.

The ship was protected and guided by marine protoforms carved – into symbols – out of the wood whose axe-edge shape cut through the salty matter of the sea. The symbols worked a magical substitution. The substitute, as symbol, participates communicatively in the brute life, sea, from which it is extracted. Because of that communicative participation, because it knows its double origin, the dragon wood knows how to grip the sea, cope with it, deflect its onslaughts, and how not to be smashed. That was how the carver of wood served his fellow beings, with capable hands. Enormous muscles on the backs and arms of the oarsmen would otherwise have been helpless. They needed these delicate and incisive woodcarver's hands, needed this information, and they needed the dragons as helpers, to anticipate and disperse the horrors of the sea.

The carving which induces the magical substitution has not only a sheltering (or passive, apotropaic) role to play. Its role is transitive too. The carving acts in and upon the sea, cuts into the sea the shape of the human journey. Finally, the carving is a model of order, good energy in good order. It signified – even if it did not always achieve – a conquest of randomness. By its transitive action this model made sense of the hazardous sea. To the oarsmen's muscles it signalled orientation among the whirling cross-currents, the heaving labyrinthine web of high tensions between order and chaos, ship and ocean.

Thinking about artifice of this kind – the prow system is not isolated, nor need we lose sight of social implications for ourselves – one comes to have doubts about poems which conform to the scripts of subjective expression; doubts also about anecdotal or confessional poems, poems that catalogue impressions additively, and so forth. I say doubts, but the key to value in any text is the character (quality) of the writing; so perhaps I have simply crept a long way around in order to concede an obvious distinction. This would be a distinction between two kinds of text, the configural and the confessional. Either may appeal to sound aesthetic judgement. If my doubts apply at all, it would be because the (broadly) confessional mode is more apt to encourage limp, self-indulgent, and haphazard writing, also because it makes room for what is fake.

The scripts for self-expression are not all formulae, not by any means. The liberating force of poetry as we know it today derives much from volcanic expressions of the recent past. From Whitman to Artaud – crises in the guts, psyche and voice, oceanic feeling, democracy, elaborate invention of human interiors, not excluding the anguish of Artaud's anus. The great confessional crowing, at its most intense, can show what reckless and savage stuff a creative individual is made of. But the artificer poets, unlike the unwinders of intestines or excavators of the void, are connected with historic places. At the very roots and altogether transparently they are connected with specific places, solid scenes. I wonder if their sense of dwelling along a particular time/space axis implies an imagination akin to that of the prow-carver.

Propertius, Musil, Lorca, Kafka, Baudelaire, Mandelstam, Balzac, Fontane, Joyce, Mörike, Proust, Leopardi, Pindar, and Ladislas Nowak in Trebic today, or Fritzi Mayröcker in her Zentagasse room – they are anything but milieu writers. They all wrestle, respectfully, with arbitrariness. Their cities, landscapes, and rooms are not photographically literal. Never frontal reportage about apparent localities, their writings are formal creations which enshrine and radiate poetic space. A particular time/space axis, as 'world of appearance', may be recognized, certainly, in the words and the imagination words embody. But that embodiment includes a crucial moment of change. Nothing is neutral any more, all is transvalued and animated by the rhythms of a unique formal vision grounded in an original sensibility. (There are many women among such writers; their keen and rich sense of space, oddly, is less mixed with artifice.)

Mörike's Swabia, Propertius's Rome, René Char's Vaucluse, all are structures – or I should say structurings – which relate transitively to the extraneous world whose form they gaily enshrine. Hence we experience these places as *world*, as *cosmos*, once we have experienced them in these forms of words. The inaugural word-forms are distinct from expression in the usual sense; they are vocal, but not thought/feeling arbitrarily vociferated. Almost they put us in perceptual contact with being; almost we perceive, in their organization, being as most subtle and integral form. It does not matter much whether the point of contact is a gutter or a fountain, a 'ship under sail' or 'a hog in a high wind', as Byron said. Perhaps the actual place, in all its dense psychic variety, was in the last analysis a focus for the creation of a vision: a vision of being as an enigmatic and deep structuring, a structuring full of conflict, but pervasive.

At which point I hear my academic hat whistling through the air, aiming to clamp itself back on my head. Yet, if I emphasize structure as a radical linguistic happening, if I consider that some structurings imply magic, I do not advocate making structure conspicuous or exclusive. No neo-Parnassian frigidity. Any doctrinaire purism repels me, even that of Gerhard Rühm. I do admire some French poets who are working intelligently to deregulate the sentence-mechanism, who have a fine sense of fragmentariness, and who rid a text of random feeling. But keep at arm's length, I tell myself, the attractive idea of a non-discursive, trans-reflexive poetry which, as it presents complex lyrical experience, is said to be a disclosure of being. At arm's length – partly because this idea lends itself to academic word-spinning, partly because conscious effort so to write results in an esotericism both vacant and prim.

All I have tried to do in these notes is propose, as one possible model for the poem, the significant and useful ancient artifact. In doing so, I stand by figurative speech, as a time-tested access to truth in finite existence, and more, as speech which tells of the impact of the world upon the body. Figures offer an access – to truth and to death – which might be called physiognomical, because it does not shear away feeling and randomness, but admits them, whatever the pain, in a purged and dynamic condition. Purged and dynamic: it is the evolving structure which, as you write your artifact into life, tests and tempers this or that feeling, this or that random particle. The testing and tempering is what eventually makes a text radiant, polysemous, and redeems it from the flat modes of confessional anecdotage or impression-cataloguing.

It is understandable that in the Bundesrepublik younger poets should place imagination, the source of figures, under suspicion (or arrest?), because of its erratic tonal flights and its deceptiveness. Understandable too, but less so for me, that in England not only younger poets seem to regard imagination much as their forebears regarded sex, as a release not often permitted, and then only if it helps you to feel better. Imagination, precisely because it is deceptive and demonic, needs artifice, needs the pressure of craft, the pleasure of artistry, for a dialectical counterpart. As another set of controls one can practise the critique of imagination suggested by Wen I, the Chinese Ch'an (Zen) master of the 10th century: 'All appearances lack in essence and all names arise from that which is nowhere.'

So the world is tottering and still you do what you can to make the prow that shall make sense of the sea, with all the times of your life and of your fellowbeings to propel the ship it guides and shields. Let subjectivity rip, in a poetry of panic and egomaniacal delirium – and the volatile, animated word, the figural form, as an aperture upon being, will very likely be splintered.

1978

2

(See References for a list of exhibits and texts which illustrated the lecture on which this part of the essay was based: prehistorical figurines and tools, Arabic, Kufic, and Greek calligraphy, pictures by Kandinsky, Klee, Malevitch, Hartung, and Carlfriedrich Claus, typography by Iliazd, concrete poems, a Rilke manuscript, and inscriptions on walls in Facteur Cheval's 'Palais Idéal'.)

These exhibits and texts are not aired in order to exemplify anything. I wanted simply to show two sets of signs with which an imagination might play, after it had been taken by the thought that between text and artifact a theoretical relation might exist, and that this relation might not interfere with tedious old distinctions between the fine, the verbal, and the useful arts. If you study Rimbaud's poem, 'Marine', you notice that an invention in words can come close to realizing an artifact model. In this case the model would be the process of braiding. Braiding goes into hair, furniture, metalwork, bread, clothing, and so on. Rimbaud was braiding images of sea and land, prow and plough, forest and jetty.

But then a model is not devised for realization; it is a theoretical construct. In the froth of phenomena models keep disappearing. Another matter to be remembered is this: As we attend to texts, things, artifacts, making and writing, we are like refugees frightened and baffled by real dangers. We look at the exhibits and see all around these limpid inventions the opaque times we are living in. Our time is the second or third phase in the age of reproducibility of works of art and of the mass replication, for commercial ends, of what George Kubler called prime objects.[1] Years ago, Walter Benjamin mapped the new situation – 'loss of aura'.[2] What troubles us now is the likelihood that some sort of vacuum, having eroded the presences of original things, artifacts and handiworks, is eating away the awesome reality of individual human lives. Adjoining Benjamin's map of the developing terrain there are terrible regions like that around the filing cabinet in chapter 1 of György Konrad's novel, *The Case Worker*. Around that cabinet there are stupefying regions crammed with futile objects that constitute no clear cut world at all, only a 'hieroglyphic pattern of...murderous devices'.[3] The totally politicized world, with its economic imperatives, grievances, greeds, is punctured all over by ideological syringes that suck and pump singularity out of everything, and flood, with embalming fluids, every vein of difference, every muscle of human oddity.

A nightmare of designification is running its course. This understood, we should consider, not without pangs and qualms, how down the centuries since somebody told how the shield of Achilles was made, poets have learned from significant things about the naming of such things and significations. They learned how essential the right words are, particularizing or flighted, words like shingle, lip, spandril, dovetail, tuft, byssus, garboard strake, topsail, stitch, clerestory, burdock, or the beautiful Greek *sphrinx*. By observing things and contemplating them steadily, they came to see things in the making, and to know how craftsmen go to work on things. They understood things as messages telling how things are made, the thing telling of its own generative process, not just a dead end-product. Some poets, like Gérard de Nerval, madly or not, also recognized in a set of material objects the play of id-forces, a universal dreamwork, their own inmost soul-drama crystallizing, puzzling itself out, in the thing or in the fluid webs of things. The regard resting on the object is thus, as sometimes in Kurosawa's films,[4] the key to self-affirmation: a self reclaims itself from nonentity and, as the object reveals itself in a certain light, that self can gaze into its own depths as an agent of interiority, no longer a mere blob to be pushed around in a flat world. Between 'I am' and 'This is' there can be strange ligatures – a magico-grammatical tissue links first and third persons singular.

In Gerard Manley Hopkins' journals[5] (1860s) there are prose studies of the distinctive forms of things (inscapes), in which the prose itself is a signature of the designing force that Hopkins called instress. Studying the way an oak tree evolves, as a unified design, he instresses into the grain of his prose the oak's gnarled and rooty gestalt. (His study of a bluebell is a brilliant exegesis of the flower's gestalt – but then Hopkins could read the flower as a sacred text.) A surprise in this area – Kipling's travel letters.[6] Kipling is invariably specific, at times a bit careless, but always curiously mixing metaphor and fact, actualizing, together with the design of the thing he presents, the delicacy and force of his perception of it. His prose goes all the way around the thing. The thing is shown as a decisive event in consciousness, as language.

All the same, a text is not in itself a thing. In some ways it is the reverse of a thing. It may be about a thing, embrace a thing and make intimate to thought a thing's hidden vital sense. But I'm trying now to look past the fascination of poems about things,[7] poems in which, as in Mörike, Rilke, and Williams, verbal design mimes an extrinsic concrete thing or kinetic grouping of things, but mimes in such a way as to melt reference into wording of high intrinsic interest. The miming would not be thinkable, let alone interesting, were it not for the fact that, even when typeface and lay-out are enlisted, as in cummings, text is nonidentical with thing. This non-identity is perfectly obvious, but it matters a good deal to the distinction that also has to be made between text and artifact.

An intelligible inscription on an artifact, a painting or a bowl, contributes to the artifact's thinginess, but is not itself a thing. In cases where a phrase or letter has been shredded and attached as graphic element to a material surface, as in Franz Mon's 'Abstraktion', we might think of the whole outcome as a thing, or, more specifically, as an artifact. But we cannot fail to recognize that the verbal-graphic element is contributive only, not self-sufficient, in the ensemble of that artifact. For millennia, inscriptions have been adjuncts to the presences of things. In this century, and before it, alphabets and syllabaries have been plundered by artists for graphic and calligraphic ends and put into pictures or upon objects that we can think of as being things. Yet we do not think of language as a thing. After all, language is not made by the hands, and it has a weird way of moving around in the body-mind, not occupying a fixed position outside it.

We also call a book a thing, but the texts which compose the book are not thought of as things (except in some such special sense as that of Francis Ponge). The book has its three dimensions, like a cup or a tombstone, you can handle it, but does a text 'have' anything at all? A Chinese scroll,

292

Tutankhamun's lotiform chalice, or Ian Hamilton Finlay's glass sheet with words sandblasted into it – these are things. But the moment those words, ideograms, or hieroglyphs, are detached from their tangible vehicle and appear as themselves alone, they re-enter the open field of non-things, non-artifacts.

A verbal design so well wrought, or so spontaneous, that it enables a reader to feel the 'very feel' of a thing, is still not itself a thing, we say. The extrinsic thing out there, or the feeling for it, is actually reinvented in the instrumentation of language called a poem. Besides, the 'very feel' comes about only through this or that unique instrumentation, which mediates the arousal of the poet in the presence, memory, or imagination, of his thing, even when the pull of the thing is reversed by the poem. All this is representation, and the textual design holds up a representation as an unbinding of the spell of idolatry. The text is an image, if you like, even when it may strain to be transparent. From the extrinsic thing the text that unbinds the spell and measures the depth of the writer's arousal is lifted by an interpreting touch. I do say lifted by an interpreting touch, because the intervention need be by no means as vast and divinatory as, say, Rilke's gaze on the head of Amenophis IV in a Berlin museum. 'Feel', he wrote to Benvenuta, 'feel from this face what it means to confront the infinite world and in a surface thus confined, through the intensified ordering of a few features, to form a counterweight to the whole manifest universe.'[8]

Rilke had more to say (and this was before he met Benvenuta and started to address her extravagantly). He wrote: 'Could not one turn away from a night sky full of stars and find in this face the same law blossoming, the same magnitude, depth, inexhaustibility to thought? From things like this I learned to see.' Extreme as this sounds, surely the delight a reader can experience in textual design, a delight with roots going down deep into his creaturely fear and trembling, comes about as a dawn of insight across this distance between star and face, thing and text. It is a distance of non-identity, which sets intelligence free to intuit a common law between star and face. The delight liberates. A re-ordering of perceptual schemata releases intellectual energy. This energy has been wrung from the inchoate and it configures in the design of the text.

Every text is singular and so is each degree of delight in the experience of each singular reader. Singularity is the term that seems best to embrace a host of foreground and background features in the experience of delight in design. The experience is one that singularizes the agent of the experience, to start with. You are on your own. Momentarily, at least, you are set apart from engulfing things by which 'we' are *bedingt* (cf. Heidegger). Singularity here, what is more, does not mean just oddity. The word comes from the Latin root *sim-*, and the derivatives of *sim-* denote self-sameness, identity, integrity, consonance of the whole person or thing, rather than similarity (to something else) in our sense. This kind of singularity of the person who responds consonantly to design, or this singularity of the text itself that embodies the design, is never actually final. Design configures the text and marks non-identity between text and thing. Design also displaces, for the singular reader, the flat confusions formerly programmed as reality. A new identity is coming into sight, uniquely the design as such, singular, also self-renewing, re-readable, because in each performance never quite the self-same. Here, I suppose, are some of the variables implied in the young Ezra Pound's *aperçu* that a 'sense of sudden growth' is what a reader feels as he responds to a complex poetic image. Hopkins, it is true, was put out when he felt that 'instress cannot come' on account of the presence of a companion; and yet, he wrote, 'I saw the inscape though freshly, as if my eye were still growing...' The truth we are after belongs, I think, in that very growing.

The braiding design in Rimbaud's poem can also be read this way. He was braiding images of sea and land. At the same time, he was dispersing, singularizing, and reinventing the world in which, habitually and referentially, sea is perceived as sea and land as land: the pedestrian world where inertia is king and metaphor the fool. The text communicating itself as immaterial reinvention of reality forcibly delivers imagination from the tyranny of things. The text as a cosmos of signs is a system with its own controls and balances – but it is not shut off or out, nor is its deliverance from things necessarily contrived by violence, a violence at once positive and distortive. No wonder it can be argued that a certain range of signs, artifacts or texts, has sacramental value.[9] In the Zuni world, for example (a basic example), what we might comfortably call reinvention was understood as a restitution of the first creation, the dawn of being, before the big fire brought the creator's wrath. The Zuni sculptor might put no more than a notch in a small stone shaped like a horned toad. For his people, that notch in a small stone nevertheless was sign enough that the stone he had found could be identified, for sacramental use, as a horned toad left over from the primal creation.

Unlike a stone or a horned toad, the text has no weight. It has no volume and no pages. It is a memory trace of a complex and radiant kind. Even if it is discontinuous, even if it is a spectre come to drink at the pool of involuntary memory, you can summon it to bring otherwise inchoate feeling into focus. The text as a non-dimensional, mental event is also a sign that in non-identity a freedom is available. Certainly your first delight is free to modulate, in quality, in its own way. Should you forget about the text, your delight is free to die. Dying, it may transform itself into a component of your general feeling. Severed from its first occasion, this delight can persist in your capacity for delight generally, in the delight you cathect into the world you are full of. It seasons your sensibility, and you can converse with it. Perhaps it opens, as an intelligible design, your mind to yourself. Formal closure of some kind might well be the mark of a text and of an artifact; at least a good sense of limit was the mark of societies neither madly classical nor madly self-destructive. Yet closure in the design of a text is not only what stimulates the sense of growth for a reader; it is also the measure of how, on some levels of signification, a text is branching out into the unknown, ramifying toward or out of the unsayable.

One step more, beyond the humanistic solecisms, then I mean to draw back and look around. Perhaps a text in all its singularity, as a dematerialization of thing into sign, as a structured but not rigid event in consciousness, with a design as fine as that of an artifact, but not identical with any artifact or thing, might show you a way toward an otherwise shuttered world of infinite delight that you carry around with you, gnash your teeth as you may. But I would not insist that the immateriality of any text points the way to a private door into 'divine nature', the private door which St. Augustine[10] said was intrinsic to each soul, and beyond which, for the soul, 'all things come to nought'. The reverse might be the case. Textual design in sedated self-destructive societies may often imply cushioning devices that absorb the shock of unholy terrors in the thing-bewitched world. That is the trouble.

Now to look around a little. How do these ideas relate to the idea of the artifact as model for a poetic text? I have proposed that you can talk back to a text which you have experienced with delight. You can also talk to a thing. Yet a thing is mute. So when you do talk to it, you are not talking back to it. You are talking to yourself through the circuitry of the thing. Or you might be talking vicariously to other people not present. (If language originated in the furious urge to communicate with onself, not with other people, then other people too are originals.)

Does what Heidegger called 'the heavenly' talk to itself vicariously through us, or through our artifacts? A tall thought, and we are little informed about this. If things are mute to us, must our artifacts be mute to angels? Rilke did not think so, in the ninth Duino Elegy. There he insisted: 'Show him (the angel of the Elegies) a thing', and 'Tell him things'.

Rilke's figurative hyperboles here cannot be transposed on to a practical level, in a designified world, without a dimming of their suggestive power. They might bring pangs of despair to people less eloquent than he, or less intimate with things than an old woman who makes rhythmic speeches to her dog and can talk to God about her knitting, as well as vice versa. Any 'angelic' illumination is made problematic, or is indefinitely postponed, by the existence of things in a world of subjectivity that is inexhaustibly self-reflexive. In Kafka nothing grows toward illumination. It is things, with their inscrutable penumbra, that spellbind the self-reflexive subject and eclipse illumination with anxiety. This human *Bedingtsein* is figured in a gigantic newspaper, a closet of whips, a cart in the corner of a nocturnal courtyard, or in Fraülein Bürstner's utterly ordinary pincushion. Thus *bedingt*, people wander around like zombies, not even knowing that is what they are, crowding history's corridors, erratic, obstructed, crushed. Kleist too seems to have thought of things as entangled fractions whirling in the vortex of erratic subjective actions. Seldom are his things stable reference points that might measure the deeper pulsations of a psyche, or might help the will to achieve some degree of orientation, retrieve the lost lucidity of instinct. St. Augustine, also Meister Eckhart, and indeed the main East-West metaphysical tradition, with its roots in the oldest strata of human self-consciousness, are intent on extricating the soul from the damnation of things, extricating it too from the gravitational force we put around things and call beauty.

So consistent is this, that one might almost think the artisanal traditions of the world were plain contrary from the start, that the metaphysicians were right, and that with materialism East or West, whoever owns the means of production, people have got what they deserved – rockets, egomania, TV dinners, and rotten operas for light relief. Even if this were not the case, puritanical fanaticism in the West has done its spiteful worst to replace things with nothing. Even the Platonic-Buddhist strain in Western poetic idioms tends to subvert the artisanal contrariness, with a few exceptions, Keats for one. (It is noticeable that in our time Williams and Ponge are distinctly anti-Platonic, Brecht too, who had a passion for old handtools, and knives and forks.) If Goethe and Wordsworth differ here, Goethe still cannot be seen as an undeviating critic of the metaphysical tradition. The old pagan is always on the lookout for archetypal 'bleibende Verhältnisse', transcendent paradigms. On 9 October, 1786, in Venice, he writes à propos shellfish: 'What a delightful, glorious thing a living entity is! How well adapted to its conditions, how true, how being!' Six months later, in Naples, à propos Rousseau, he writes: 'If I didn't have such sympathy with things of nature, or see that there are ways of sorting out and comparing hundreds of observations despite the apparent confusion – as a surveyor does when with a single straight line he checks many separate measurements – I should often think I was mad myself.'[11] Time and again Goethe's fantastic sympathy for things in nature compels him to sing them to sleep for a while, so that he can speculate about entelechies (in paintings he also looks for the story-line). We should note: Had he subtracted from the irreducible singular thing his feeling of partnership with it, or his abstractive gaze upon it, either way that thing in the immediate confusion of things could for him have been more like a knocker on the gate of a madhouse, than a latch on the soul's private door into 'divine nature'.

Now it is intriguing that we should except writings from our categories of things. Horrendously rugged proto-Germans may have had some such word as 'dinc'. By 'dinc' their successors meant 'assembly', possibly too the common concern, focusing event or crisis, which might occasion the elders of a group to reason together. The Latin 'res' had originally the same sense. In neither case was the word for thing applied in our narrower sense, to particular external objects. It almost looks as if an old semantic muddle, or else a fabulous psychological transformation, underlies our reluctance to think of a significant text as a 'thing' belonging in the orders of prophetic dreams, invasions, oracles, incest, or famine.

French 'chose', similarly, comes from Latin 'causa', again the word for a concern, and for a case (like German 'Sache'), but not, it seems, for cause in the sense of ground (German 'Ursache'). Heidegger plots these etymologies and prefers, for his priceless speculations on a jug, an ancient sense of thing as 'gathering'.[12] He also carried across into them the sense of Greek 'on', Latin 'ens', as 'that which is present ... put here, put before us, presented'. He does not refer to Sanskrit levels of Indo-European.

Etymology gives us a glimpse behind current usage, but still we are in the dark as regards which word prehistoric speakers might have used, if ever they wanted to pronounce sounds in order to refer non-specifically to such things as 'stone', 'shaft', or later 'hoe', and 'pick'. Perhaps there was no non-specific word. If there was none, how should we think about events in the mind of a typical prehistoric speaker, who might never have been able to say: 'Look, northward, what is that thing out there?'

It is possible that such a person, for all his amazing skills and other powers of communication, linguistic powers included, lacked any organ to locate and identify natural objects or artifacts as 'entities' altogether *separate* from his own person. Discussion in our terms becomes doubly difficult if you think that he might have thought of his own

298

person not as 'I' but as 'he'. Only, perhaps, with the accumulation of spare things, in a world that had marched away from subsistence economy, a world with power-centralization and property, a world that had shifted from right hemisphere to left hemisphere thinking, a world with a grammar that arose with the neural shift away from magical thinking toward cortical or subjective thinking, did a term as non-specific as 'thing' in our sense enter ancient man's vocabulary.

Only then, again perhaps, did a later variant of 'dinc' come into use as a term with which to designate a discrete, exterior, objective, manipulable entity, separate from consciousness, but serving it – a genuine *Gegenstand*. In this case, the notion 'thing', as object, comes to life along with individual self-consciousness, as contrasted to group-consciousness. It comes to life with the breakdown of some very ancient magical cohesion, in which mind had been a shared social coagulant, and not really subjective – here I'm leaning on Julian Jaynes's set of arguable hypotheses.[13] It comes to life with trade between magically coherent societies, if it was trade (besides vast geophysical catastrophes and difficult encounters between foreigners) that transformed, or shattered, the unconscious semantic bonds that kept those societies discrete and insulated. Far back, one might speculate, the concept 'thing' is already to be linked with diversification, economics, alienation, and finally reification.

Bleak thought: the word once still used to signify a common concern now signifies objects for which we compete, over which we squabble, with which we pretend to be on top and well off, commodities replicating themselves *ad infinitum*, jealously guarded acquisitions, cold comforters for our slowly powdering bones. Yet even in our sense certain things have retained some of their ancient energy. Out of things, and quite especially out of artifacts, we can still draw the fine fugitive tunes and harmonies of consciousness as language. Even if we no longer construct Gothic cathedrals, some things, even good cars, can still embody for us the intellectual and social configurations which linguistic interpretations of them convoke.

Other things do gather the rays of feeling with which we – in our indelibly animistic afterthoughts – pretend to penetrate them, and they reply to those rays with presence. Briefly, even when things retain their trans-linguistic purity in silence, they are essential to our social and private coherences; and our artifacts do encode those coherences in peculiarly transparent ciphers. To go back to the contrary old artisans: they were right. They did not contradict spirit really. They were designing spaces in which spirit, on its adventures, might call in, or rest awhile, after shaking hands with a few people. Or else they really did contradict spirit, and that contradiction was just what spirit was calling for, because spirit needed to be provoked – paradox was the condition of its appearing.

Artifacts are highly organized, distinct, and subtle things. Contemplate a Yurok basket, try to embrace its intricate formal weave as well as the skill and work that have 'gone into it'. The contemplator and the thing conspire to bring matter back into the spontaneous motives of thought, to retrieve matter into the rumorous life of reflection, deliver matter from separateness while not violating its difference. A text, as a mental event, as a common concern, is also an ensign that convokes us and even emboldens us in the fight for interior life. It is, to this extent, just as provocative as an artifact can be, even if its status, that of the text, is unstable, or liminal, itinerant between interiority and externals, the imaginable and the actual, the silence and the speaking.

What is this will to retrieval? Is it a real function of so-called intentionality in a text as work of art? Intentionality might be the fiat which sets certain elements loose in play; as that play becomes determinate as text, the elements configure into a design, and that design asserts, like an arrow shot from a bow in perfect tension, the central fact of language, which is relation. I think this may be so. But I can think of many texts that just do not do what I say they are meant to do. The fundamental notion here is that intentionality institutes play first, the determinations only later. A Yurok basketmaker, too, is quoted as saying: 'While basketweaving sit with your back to the fire. Do not think of it as hard work or the basket will not be good.'[14]

Yet this fiat of intentionality, also this retrieval, are what a reader can feel when the text is before him, growing into his world as he grows into its world. This is what he feels when this text, as artifact, 'res', or 'dinc' or imagination,

300

defies and dissolves the fossil codes, those determinate yet so slippery things out there, the fictions we institutionalize in our fear and with our all-entombing idolatry. Without demonstrating anything, a text can at least recall to us our gifts of being free, singular, and grateful. This in-stance of the text as a thing presented, though not a thing, as a thing recovered into thought and shining anew with the aureole of thought that gave birth to it, this very nearness of the text to its own origination restores to us the feel of distance, our own distance, for it is we who are performing that text and closing that distance.

The distance which is performed as a closing is recognized as the afterglow of a design, because an optimum response to a textual design is going out from the person reading. I go out first as regards the text as an alien external. Then, as regards that text's intrinsic radiation, I go out toward the whole field of reference and connotation it projects – its 'thing'. The in-stance of the text and the distance to the thing are convoked by the authority of a linguistic design alone. In-stance and distance are dialectical co-ordinates that regulate a reader's responses as he reads, they are his fabulous or plain frame of interpretation. They continue to nourish his general responsiveness thereafter. The freedom of non-identity modulates into the freedom of self-discovery, and then into the freedom of this going out from person to the thing invoked by the text. In this transaction, it is not so much the person of the artificer that counts. What counts is the authority with which that person has invested the textual design, an authority behind which he stands. That authority in the design laughs at the comical set of contrivances called 'person'.

Finally, it would seem that this kind of design, which attunes and regulates the text, inconspicuous as it may be, also this experience for the reader, are peculiar to lyric utterance rather than any other. Conceivably they might help us to fathom some of the ways in which lyric utterance can, in one fell swoop, invoke a spirit and be radiant with bodiliness. Apostrophe, the invocation of a spirit, though now archaic, is still fundamental to the lyric in one form or another. Mörike modulated the old spirit-invoking apostrophe into the thou-address of his poem 'Auf eine Lampe'. Rilke, before he could modulate from his juvenile Ah and

301

Oh of *Das Stundenbuch* to the questing celebrations and invocations of the Elegies and Sonnets, had to discipline his whole imagination toward 'sachliches Sagen' – concretely realizing utterance – which he found as exemplary pictorial presence in Cézanne. In both poets there is respect for the thing with its distance, respect for the design as in-stance, and respect for the perfection of the text that sustains caprice as a vital factor in design but delivers design from the flipflop of subjective randomness.

My theme of poem and artifact was provoked by a picture of a Viking prow, as the prow came out of the mud and before it was restored. Rimbaud's 'Marine' kept other thoughts in motion, thoughts about the poetic reinvention of reality. I am still haunted by a third sea image. Xenophon, in the *Anabasis*, describing the situation of the Greeks as they struggled out of Asia, along the Euxine coast, and across into Thrace, mentions a headland on which, after a shipwreck, a book might be washed ashore. The book would have been on its way eastward, to a Greek colonial city, perhaps into the possession of a Crimean barbarian learning Greek. But it was washed ashore, along with other artifacts in the cargo, wooden beds, oars, chests of oak or olive wood. The book's pages, of papyrus or goatskin parchment, would have been soaked, its wooden covers stained and warped by the sea. Once it reached land, the wind might have riffled the pages and dried them. The text, though blurred, was still not unclear – perhaps a play, or a dialogue, or a song. Suppose an illiterate beachcomber picked it up and took a look: what use or meaning could the book have had for him? Or else this book was not rescued. It fell apart, became débris, among seashells, the shit of gulls, pearly like their feathers, and other changeful artifacts of nature, epiphanies of chance. Three angles for a fix on cosmogenesis: a book disintegrating into the Bosphorus; a text, not lost, Xenophon, the only reminder of it; and ourselves in this moment, remembering the sound the book made as it fell through the air, when the beachcomber let it drop.

1979

302

Details of slides and texts illustrating the lecture as which this essay began: SB = reproduced from *Schrift und Bild*, catalogue, Frankfurt am Main, Typos Verlag, for Staatliche Kunsthalle, Baden-Baden, 1963; CP = reproduced from *Concrete Poetry: a world view*, edited by Mary Ellen Solt, Bloomington, Indiana University Press, 1968.

1. Prow of Oseberg Viking ship before restoration.
2. Early Stone Age amber figurines (National Museum of Denmark).
3. Late Stone Age flint dagger imitating form of bronze dagger, from Funen, Denmark (1800-1500 BC).
4. Christ Divine Wisdom (painting, Byzantine Museum, Athens – Christ holding Bible open in his left hand).
5. Two figure-painted playing cards, with ideogram texts, from a set used for poetic guessing games. Early 12th c. Japan (University of Durham, Gulbenkian Museum).
6. Persian calligraphy, proverb in shape of a bird, AD 1872 (SB).
7. Kufic script (visual-lexical calligraphy) (SB).
8. Hans Hartung, *Encre de chine*, 1952 (calligraphy as abstract picture) (SB).
9. Codex Alexandrinus. Greek script on vellum, 5th c. AD (British Museum).
10. Vassily Kandinsky, *Rows of Symbols*, 1931 (painting, Kunstsammlung, Basel).
11. Wally Barker, *Brown Watercolour*, 1961. (SB).
12. I.C. Hiltensperger (master calligrapher), *Labyrinth*, early 18th c. (calligraphy in rotation) (SB).
13. Ferdinand Kriwet, *Rundscheibe Nr.5*, 1962 (print in rotation) (SB).
14. Paul Klee, *Er küsse mich*, 1921 (picture-text from Song of Songs (SB).
15. Paul Klee, *Ad marginem*, 1930-36 (isolated letters in painting, Kunstsammlung, Basel).
16. Paul Klee, *Anfang eines Gedichtes*, 1938 (scattered childish letters assembling) (SB).
17. Carlfriedrich Claus, *Paracelsische Denklandschaft*, 1962 (imaginary language picture-text) (SB).

18. Kasimir Malevitch, *Englishman in Moscow*, 1913-14 (Russian letters as elements in design, painting, Amsterdam) (SB).
19. Iliazd (Ilya Zdanevitch), page from *Ledentu, le phare* (play), 1923 (Russian typographic invention) (SB).
20. Jiří Kolář, *Le poème évident*, 1967 (picture/wording collage) (CP).
21. Ian Hamilton Finlay, *Wave/Rock*, 1966 (printed words sandblasted into glass, photo by Jonathan Williams) (CP).
22. Franz Mon, *Abstraktion*, 1963 (shredded letters) (SB).
23. Rilke, autograph of last Orpheus Sonnet, 1923.
24. Facteur Cheval, interior wall of his Palais Idéal, with inscription (Hauterives, SE France, c.1910).

Texts
1. Arthur Rimbaud, 'Marine' (from *Les Illuminations*, c. 1872-74).
2. Gerard Manley Hopkins, journal for 11 July, 1866.
3. Eduard Mörike, 'Auf eine Lampe' (1846), 'Im Park' (Spring 1847).
4. Rudyard Kipling, from *Letters of Travel* (The Canadian Pacific, 1892).
5. Rainer Maria Rilke, 'Römische Fontäne' (July 1906), 'Der Ball' (July 1907).
6. William Carlos Williams, 'The Term', *Spring and All*, XXI, 'Poem' ('As the cat...') (1920s).
7. Poem by e.e. cummings.

References in the text
1. George Kubler, *The Shape of Time* (Yale University Press, 1962).
2. Walter Benjamin, 'Das Kunstwerk im Zeitalter seiner technischen Reproduzierbarkeit' (1935), in *Illuminationen* (Frankfurt am Main: Suhrkamp Verlag, 1961).
3. George Konrad, *The Case Worker* (Harcourt Brace, 1974) p. 18; cf. p. 86 – 'In the phantasmagoric world of good and evil, ... in that ambiguous heedless world of ideas that has no more relevance to the massive ambiguity of human affairs than an impotent old man to the backside of a whore, I have stood with the judges for as long as I can remember, but... far from wholeheartedly.'

4. On Kurosawa: Dennis Giles, 'Kurosawa's Heroes', in *Arion* (new series), 2 (1975) 2.

5. Gerard Manley Hopkins, *Poems and Prose*, W.H. Gardner (ed.) (Penguin, 1953) 'Oak tree', p. 110, 'bluebell' pp. 122-3; 'growing', p. 129 (see below).

6. Rudyard Kipling, *Letters of Travel, 1892-1913* (Scribner, 1920) esp. pp. 30-31, e.g., 'The mountain torrent is a boss of palest emerald ice against the dazzle of the snow; the pine stumps are capped and hooded with gigantic mushrooms of snow...'

7. On some poems about things, see N.M. Willard, 'A Poetry of Things: Williams, Rilke, Ponge' in *Comparative Literature*, 17, 1965. An admirable but little known essay on things and poems – which I had not read before writing mine, is Gregor Sebba's 'Das Kunstwerk als Kosmion' in *Politische Ordnung und menschliche Existenz: Festgabe für Eric Voegelin*, Alois Dempf, Hannah Arendt, and Friedrich Engel-Jacobi (eds.) (Munich: C.H. Beck, 1962).

8. Rilke on Amenophis IV, in Magda von Hattingberg, *Rilke und Benvenuta* (Vienna, 1947) p. 282.

9. *Sacramental value*: see David Jones, 'Art and Sacrament' in his *Epoch and Artist* (Faber, 1959).

10. Saint Augustine, quoted by Meister Eckhart, in *The Spear of Gold* H.A. Reinhold (ed.) (Burns Oates, 1947) p. 60.

11. Goethe, *Italienische Reise* Hamburger Ausgabe, XI (1950 and 1957) pp. 93 and 211. The Mayer-Auden translation of the 9 October passage is weak (and wrong), so I have not adopted it. I modify for accuracy their translation of the later passage: *Italian Journey*, translated by W.H. Auden and Elizabeth Mayer (Collins, 1962) pp. 84 and 202.

12. Martin Heidegger, 'The Thing' in *Poetry, Language, Thought*, translated by Albert Hofstadter (New York: Harper & Row, 1971), p. 176. Heidegger oddly ignores the Sanskrit word *vastu*, which is polysemous, meaning 'abiding essence', 'subject of concern', 'object', 'property'. See Sir Monier Monier-Williams, *Sanskrit-English Dictionary*. (Oxford: Clarendon Press, 1899) p. 932. The word vástu (accented *a*) means 'becoming light', 'dawning', 'morning'. It is possible that this sense coincides

with the 'abiding essence' of vástú (equal accent)? Did the latter's sense, as 'object', arise by analogy out of 'abiding essence', but at a later date? The words might be related, within a preliterate, pre-selfconscious semantics of 'disclosure', so that at a certain stage in the evolution of consciousness a thing could be experienced as an opening on being, a dawn of being. This sense seems to be preserved in Greek *phainomenon*, and is tacit even in German *Erscheinung*.

13. Julian Jaynes, *The Origin of Consciousness in the Breakdown of the Bicameral Mind.* (Houghton Mifflin, 1976).
14. Yurok saying: Sandra Corrie Newman, quoting Rea Barber, in *Indian Basket Weaving* (Flagstaff: Northland Press, 1974) p. 25.